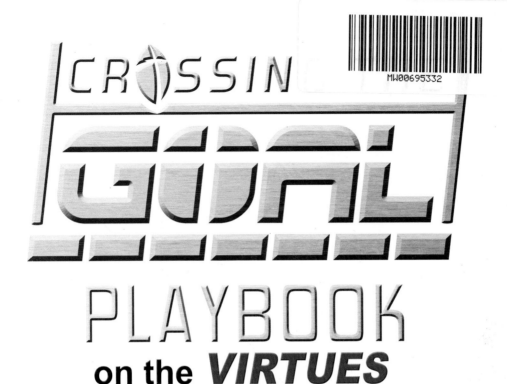

PLAYBOOK
on the VIRTUES

PLAYBOOK
on the *VIRTUES*

EMMAUS
ROAD
PUBLISHING

Steubenville, Ohio
A Division of Catholics United for the Faith
www.emmausroad.org

Danny Abramowicz • Peter Herbeck
Brian Patrick • Curtis Martin

Emmaus Road Publishing
827 North Fourth Street
Steubenville, Ohio 43952

Library of Congress Control Number: 2009925318
ISBN: 9781931018548

Cover design and layout by
Theresa Westling

CONTENTS

ONLINE EXCLUSIVE!

- How to ask questions that encourage discussion.

- How to keep the discussion on track.

- How to keep everyone involved.

LEADING A DISCUSSION

Look for these and other tips at
emmausroad.org
for Leading a Discussion!

STARTING FORMATION

It's time to get in position.

First, sit quietly, and empty all the distractions out of your mind.

Now, fold your hands in front of you and talk to God.

You probably know the Our Father and some other favorite prayers. But maybe you just need to talk to God, man to man, like a friend. Here's a prayer from our coach, Danny Abramowicz:

> Lord, change me.
> Help me.
> I'm struggling down here.
> Please help me.

You don't have to use those words, although you can if you want to. Just tell God what's on your mind.

If you're having trouble with family, ask God to help you with that.

If you're wrestling with addictions, ask God for strength.

If things seem to be falling apart, and you want to know what you're doing wrong, ask God to tell you.

If you have doubts, ask God to strengthen your faith.

Remember that Jesus taught us to call His Father, *our* Father. When Jesus showed us how to pray, He used simple language. We don't have to be great orators to pray. We just have to have problems we need help with.

And there's not one of us who hasn't got problems.

HOW TO USE THIS PLAYBOOK

This playbook is designed to help you get more from the show Crossing the Goal than you could if you just watched the show with a group of friends.

You can use the book on your own, of course. It will help you think about what you heard on the show, and apply it all to your own life.

But the playbook is even better with a group of men. As our friends on the show point out over and over, it really helps to have friends to talk with about these things.

There's a lot to talk about in each episode. The show really lends itself to discussion groups. But it's sometimes hard to remember exactly what was said in a show, even five minutes after it's over.

So, this playbook has a brief summary of the main points in each show. It also has some background information to help you get more out of the show and some suggestions for discussion to help get you started talking.

Before you watch an episode, you might want to read the "Pre-Game" section for that episode. It's not necessary but it might help you think about some of the things you'll hear about in the show.

If you miss an episode (or the entire series), this playbook has enough content from the show to be used on its own.

Each show is divided into four parts:

1. KICKOFF

This is where we look at the problem of the day. What is the problem, and what does it affect in our lives?

2. GAME PLAN

Here we learn the facts. We define the virtue we need to grow in, and we talk about the dangers and temptations that try to keep us away from that virtue.

In this book, we've added a "Game Plan" Summary for each chapter—a box with a few quick points to remember.

3. THE RED ZONE

Good advice from our friends about how they've dealt with these problems in their own lives.

4. THE END ZONE

A few last words of wisdom from each of the guys—practical wisdom that we can all apply to our lives.

The playbook for each episode has the same four parts. "To talk about" suggestions will help get group discussions started—or just give you things to think about on your own. Quick summaries of the main points brought up in each part of the show will be handy when you're talking or thinking.

There are spaces for you to write down your own ideas in response to these suggestions. Write down what you think of—it's easy to forget a good idea if you try to keep it in your head. You can write notes here before you discuss the question, or while you're talking about it.

We've also added a "Halftime" feature between the second and third parts of each episode in this book. This is just a bit of inspiration— a story from the Bible or the life of some great Christian. Like any halftime show, it's meant to get you pumped up and ready for the rest of the game.

COURAGE

Brian Patrick

PRE-GAME

When we think of great men, we think of people who showed real courage. But what is courage?

What do you think of when you think of courage? Is it something you're born with or something you need to work on? Does it mean the same thing as fearlessness?

Maybe it will help to consider a story of a man who showed real courage. Then we can ask ourselves what his courage was like.

Thomas More was certainly someone who showed courage. We remember him as a saint and martyr.

But More was just an average family man. Just like everyone else, he liked to be comfortable, and he appreciated success. He rose quickly through the ranks of English government to become Chancellor.

In addition to his talent in management, More was a good writer. His boss, King Henry VIII, knew he could count on More not only to run the day-to-day business of government but, also, to help him out in the big intellectual debate of the era—the conflict of Martin Luther with the Catholic Church.

Henry was on the Church's side, and so was More. (If that's not the way you remember Henry VIII, that's because we haven't got to the end of the story yet.) More helped the King write his *Defense of the Seven Sacraments,* which pleased the Pope so much that Henry was awarded the title "Defender of the Faith."

But we all know how Henry VIII turned out. When the King wanted to divorce his first wife, he persuaded the English bishops to sign a letter to the

Pope asking him to grant an annulment. (Henry could be very persuasive.) Then he demanded that More sign it, too.

More couldn't. He served the King as best as he could, but the law of Christ was higher than the law of Henry.

Now, More tried everything he could to avoid a confrontation. He resigned as chancellor on reasons of health, which meant he went from rich to middle-class at best. When Henry declared himself head of the English church, More signed an oath to recognize that claim "as far as the law of God will permit." When Henry remarried, More simply stayed away, doing everything he could to avoid a public break with the King.

But Henry pushed and pushed. He knew how much More was respected, and More's silence wasn't good enough. Henry needed More's approval. When Henry came up with an oath that More couldn't sign without betraying his principles, More went to prison. Later he was tried, convicted of treason, and beheaded.

So what did Thomas More's courage look like?

More never looked for martyrdom. He always avoided a fight with Henry when he could. He bent over backwards to find ways that he could agree with Henry and still keep his own principles.

But in the end he had to make a decision. When it came to that stark choice, More chose God's way over Henry's way. It wasn't that he enjoyed losing all his earthly goods; it was just that he knew which choice was right. By giving up what the world saw as greatness, he actually became the truly great man he was meant to be.

That's what St. Thomas More's courage was like. Not the fearless rushing-into-battle kind of courage but, rather, the last-resort kind of courage.

And perhaps that's what the Lord wants from us, too.

We're meant for greatness. But it takes courage to get there.

What keeps us from being the men we're meant to be?

KICKOFF

1. The world is radically broken. Think of abortion, pornography, divorce, etc.

2. We as men need to step up.

3. But the problem isn't just outside us. The problem is *inside* us. We spend more than we earn, we are addicted to Internet pornography, we have marriage troubles.

4. Deep inside us, there's a desire to be great. That's a call from God.

5. How do we find that greatness inside us? Two steps:
   A. *Recognize the crisis*. There *is* something out there, and it's ugly.
   B. Realize that we were made for a purpose, and that purpose is *to become great*.

6. Our whole culture keeps us distracted—keeping us from looking inside.

7. We need to stop to look inside. The voice of God is inside us.

8. We want to be great, but we also want to be comfortable. You can't be both. You have to get outside your comfort zone and push yourself.

9. The voice within us wants to tell us who we are; that we were made for greatness. That interior conversation can give us the hope and confidence we need to respond to the challenges we face.

10. We need to have some quiet time to listen to that voice.

CALLED TO GREATNESS

But you are a chosen race, a royal priesthood, a holy nation, God's own people, that you may declare the wonderful deeds of him who called you out of darkness into his marvelous light. Once you were no people but now you are God's people; once you had not received mercy but now you have received mercy. (1 Peter 2:9–10)

To talk about:
What are the biggest distractions in our lives? What pulls us away from the goal and keeps us from living up to our potential greatness?

- Television: How many hours a day is the television on in our houses? Could we enjoy that time more if we were doing something else?

- Work: How many hours a week do we work? Is that work separating us from our families? Do we really need to work that much or has work become another distraction to keep us from the greatness we're really meant for? Could we get more done in less time by concentrating on the task at hand? Or do we really need to rethink the whole emphasis of our lives?

- Addictions: Drug abuse and alcoholism are big problems, but there are many other kinds of addictions, too. Shopping, making money, sex, cell phones, food—these can all be addictions. Like drugs and alcohol, they're not bad in themselves—but they can be very bad when we misuse them. They can lead us away from the goal.

3

Write down some of the biggest distractions in your life. Then write down some of the good and important things they distract you from.

_____

_____

_____

_____

_____

_____

_____

_____

_____

_____

_____

_____

_____

_____

_____

_____

_____

_____

_____

_____

GAME PLAN

1. *Fortitude,* or courage, is a willingness to sustain an injury for the sake of the good. I fear the thing I face, but I don't let the fear control my response.

2. Courage doesn't mean being without fear. It means experiencing the fear but acting anyway. You can't act courageously without experiencing fear.

3. Our lives are *not* insignificant. God created us for a purpose. *We're made to be great.*

4. A good example of courage: the firefighters on 9/11. When they walked into the smoke and flames, they felt fear but they didn't let the fear decide what they did.

5. Why would I do that?
   A. Because the Lord is the model for us. He said, "This is the way to life."
   B. Because Christian hope is real. The worst thing that could happen to me is that I could die, but *that's only temporary* if we listen to that voice inside us.

6. Our Lord said that there's no greater love than to lay your life down for your friend. If you lay your life down, *the Lord will raise it back up.* Even when we risk everything, we're not ultimately risking *anything.* We have to trust our Lord completely.

7. Courage protects us from loving our lives so much that we lose them.

8. With the virtue of courage, you not only endure trials but also endure them with joy.

9. The martyrs are good examples. Maximilian Kolbe in the concentration camp says, "I'll die in this man's place."

10. Patience, calm, serenity of soul are part of Christian courage, because we understand the deeper purpose of our lives.

WE'RE EXPECTED TO BE HEROES

This is my commandment, that you love one another as I have loved you. Greater love has no man than this, that a man lay down his life for his friends. You are my friends if you do what I command you. No longer do I call you servants, for the servant does not know what his master is doing; but I have called you friends, for all that I have heard from my Father I have made known to you. (John 15:12–15)

5

To talk about:

We may never be called on to lay down our lives for the good, but what things in our own lives take real courage to face?

- Money: Are we looking away from mounting debt that could catch up with us—even tear our families apart? Are we avoiding the painful decisions and hard sacrifices it would take to deal with the problem?
- Work: Do we ignore unethical practices where we work because it's not our department? Do we go along with things at work that our consciences tell us shouldn't happen?
- Friends: Do we smile and laugh when friends repeat malicious gossip or tell racist jokes, letting them believe by our silence that we approve? Do we let friends goad us into doing things we know we shouldn't?
- Family: Do any family members have serious troubles that we're ignoring because we're afraid of the confrontation? Have we postponed getting loved ones the help they really need because talking about it is just too unpleasant?

Write down some of the things you find hardest to deal with and why they're so hard.

GAME PLAN SUMMARY

Courage: The willingness to endure an injury for the sake of the good.

Don't be afraid of fear. Courage doesn't mean fearlessness: it means doing what's right anyway, even though you're afraid.

Remember the example of Jesus. Even though He was sweating drops of blood, He said, "Your will be done."

Keep it in perspective. The worst thing that could happen is death—and even that is only temporary.

HALFTIME

Hall of Fame Profile: Maximilian Kolbe

Prison life is never easy, but life in a Nazi concentration camp was constant torture.

The Nazis weren't just cruel. Ordinary prison guards can be cruel, but the Nazis made a science of it. They turned cruelty into standard procedure.

In the most notorious camp of all, Auschwitz, the Nazi camp administration came up with a perfectly scientific and efficient way to keep prisoners from escaping. For every one who escaped, they would kill ten of his remaining friends from the same barracks. And they wouldn't just kill them—they'd starve them to death slowly, with plenty of torture along the way.

It was typical Nazi thinking. It did the job very well, because everyone had friends or family in the same barracks. Who could bear the thought of escape knowing that ten of his loved ones would be tortured to death?

Nevertheless, one day a man went missing from one of the barracks. (Most reports say the man was later found dead in the camp latrine, but he was missing, and that was all that mattered to the Nazis.) Methodically the deputy camp commander rounded up ten men and told them they would be starved to death in the notorious Block 13.

"No!" one of the men wailed. "I have a family!"

That cry did nothing to move the pity of the Nazi officer, of course. But it did move the pity of someone else.

An unassuming middle-aged man stepped forward from among the men who hadn't been selected to die. "Excuse me," he said. "I'd like to take that man's place." He explained that he was an old priest, so he had no family to take care of.

The deputy commander was a bit surprised, but it was fine with him. As long as he had ten victims, he didn't care who they were.

So Maximilian Kolbe took the place of the young family man and went to Block 13. There the prisoners were left to starve until they died.

Kolbe led them in prayers and songs, reminding them that they would soon be with Mary and the saints. As long as any of his companions were left alive, Kolbe stayed alive. The Nazis finally got impatient and killed him with a lethal injection.

And what about the young man whose life Kolbe saved? He survived the Second World War and afterwards spent the rest of his life telling everyone what Maximilian Kolbe had done for him. He lived long enough to be present when Kolbe was canonized as a saint in 1982.

THE RED ZONE

1. We don't set the bar high enough.
2. That can be because the bar seems too high as it is. Why should we set it higher?
3. But we have a sense that we were made for something more.
4. If we keep the bar low, we live down to it.
5. Examples of setting the bar high:
   A. Danny Abramowicz demanding another chance to prove himself. He refused to quit.
   B. The Hungarian greeting-card entrepreneur who refused to do pornographic greeting cards. He took a stand. He prayed and relied on the Lord. His strength was leaning on the Lord. "I'm living to please the Lord."
6. What appear to be road blocks—we've just got to power through them.
7. There's not one of us who couldn't raise the bar a little more. That's what the world is waiting for—men to rise up and raise the bar.

8. We're tempted to say, "What's the best business move?" We've got to provide for our families. But there's a higher guide—that's got to be first.

9. You're going to feel good about yourself if you step out for the Lord. It won't be easy—don't kid yourself—but you'll feel really good the day you meet the Lord.

10. Turning our hearts to the Lord gets us out of the rut.

11. Everyone's got serious problems. Go to the Lord and ask for help.

12. You can't do it alone. You need other guys who can help you up.

EVERY ONE HELPS HIS NEIGHBOR

Every one helps his neighbor,
and says to his brother, "Take courage!"
The craftsman encourages the goldsmith,
and he who smooths with the hammer him who strikes the anvil,
saying of the soldering, "It is good";
and they fasten it with nails so that it cannot be moved.
But you, Israel, my servant,
Jacob, whom I have chosen,
the offspring of Abraham, my friend;
you whom I took from the ends of the earth,
and called from its farthest corners,
saying to you, "You are my servant,
I have chosen you and not cast you off":
fear not, for I am with you,
be not dismayed, for I am your God;
I will strengthen you, I will help you,
I will uphold you with my victorious right hand.
(Isaiah 41:6–10)

To talk about:

What really keeps us from setting the bar higher? Maybe it's one of these things:

- Worries about money—I can't give more, because I'm spending everything I earn on keeping my family together.

- Worries about time—I can't do more, because every moment of my time is taken up already.

- Worries about work—if I don't throw myself into it and work as many hours as I can, they'll find someone more dedicated to replace me.

- Worries about the future—I have enough now, but will I have enough tomorrow? Better play it safe.

Now try to think how we can overcome each of those worries. Let's ask ourselves some questions:

- Worries about money: How am I spending money now? How many things am I spending it on that I don't really need? Could I cut down on recurring expenses, like beer, or wine, or cigarettes, or double mocha latte supreme every day at the coffee shop? Do I really need all those premium channels on cable? Just saving $5 a day—say by cutting out dessert at lunch—would save $1,825 a year. Think how much good we could do with that!

- Worries about time: What am I doing with my time now? How many hours a day do I spend watching television? How much time surfing the Net aimlessly? We're all busy, but God has given us 24 hours in every day. Finding just one extra hour a day—say, by giving up one television program—would give us time to read God's Word, to be with our families, or to do those other important things we've been neglecting. A lot can be accomplished in just one hour.

- Worries about work: How efficient am I at work? Do I spend time standing around talking when I could be getting things done? By just being persistent and using time wisely, we can usually get a whole day's work done in eight hours. Or is the job one where "face time" is important? There may come a time to decide that family or church is more important than a job that demands all our time just for appearance's sake.

- Worries about the future: Remember that the future will come no matter what we do about it. We don't know what it will look like, but the important thing is that God has promised to take care of us.

Write down some of your biggest worries—the things that keep you from setting the bar higher. Then, for each one, try to write down something that would help you work through that worry.

DON'T WORRY ABOUT TOMORROW

Therefore I tell you, do not be anxious about your life, what you shall eat or what you shall drink, nor about your body, what you shall put on. Is not life more than food, and the body more than clothing?

Look at the birds of the air: they neither sow nor reap nor gather into barns, and yet your heavenly Father feeds them. Are you not of more value than they? And which of you by being anxious can add one cubit to his span of life? And why are you anxious about clothing? Consider the lilies of the field, how they grow; they neither toil nor spin; yet I tell you, even Solomon in all his glory was not arrayed like one of these.

But if God so clothes the grass of the field, which today is alive and tomorrow is thrown into the oven, will he not much more clothe you, O men of little faith? Therefore do not be anxious, saying, "What shall we eat?" or "What shall we drink?" or "What shall we wear?" For the Gentiles seek all these things; and your heavenly Father knows that you need them all. But seek first his kingdom and his righteousness, and all these things shall be yours as well.

Therefore do not be anxious about tomorrow, for tomorrow will be anxious for itself. Let the day's own trouble be sufficient for the day." (Matthew 6:25–34)

THE END ZONE

Dare to Believe

You've been called to greatness.
The Lord has the power you need to rise to that level.
The Lord loves faith and is pleased with those who trust Him.

Look into your own life

Is there an area that needs the touch of Jesus Christ?
If you apply yourself, you can make the world a better place.
That's what the world is waiting for you to do.

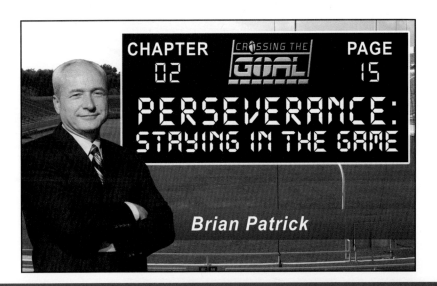

PRE-GAME

He was a young man from a good family, respectable people who expected their son to be as respectable as they were. They gave him the best education. They had a career all picked out for him.

But he was a rebel, and he didn't want the respectable life his parents had built up for him. He wanted to give it all up and take up some hippie lifestyle, living in a commune with a bunch of crazy people.

His parents didn't know what to do with him. Where had they gone wrong?

But whatever had gone wrong, they weren't going to let their son throw his life away. As the young man was heading for his new life, his brothers suddenly ambushed him, grabbed him, and took him back to the family. Whatever they did, they weren't going to let him join the Dominicans.

Yes, that was the hippie commune the young man wanted to join—the new order of Dominican friars, who were looking for the most talented minds in Europe. And the young man was Thomas Aquinas, who would certainly go on to justify the Dominicans' faith in him.

But first he had to deal with his family.

For more than a year, they kept him a prisoner against his will. At one point his brothers even brought in a prostitute, hoping they could tempt Thomas by making the comforts of this life readily available.

But Thomas wouldn't budge. He chased the woman out of the room.

His family simply didn't know what to make of him. They had such a respectable life planned out for him, and he wanted to throw it all away!

Finally, the Pope himself heard of the situation and demanded that Thomas be allowed to join the Dominicans.

We know what happened after that. Thomas became one of the most important theologians in the history of the Church, spending his life in making a systematic encyclopedia of Church doctrine.

But it would never have happened if he hadn't *persevered*. He had to endure every kind of temptation to stray from what he knew was right, even when the temptations were offered by his own family. And he had to endure it for more than a year, every single day, every hour and every minute of the day, never giving up on the courageous decision he'd made.

Perseverance is like that. It's the virtue that keeps us going, even when we're dog-tired, because we just know it would be wrong to give up. Courage helps us overcome our fear to make the tough decisions; perseverance keeps us going even after that first rush wears off and it's just a lot of work.

KICKOFF

1. Virtue is becoming what God has made us to be.

2. To get there is a battle.

3. The battle's not a sprint: it's a marathon. The one who perseveres wins.

4. We look for escapes to make the world something it's not. Alcohol, for example, can be an escape from the real world.

5. We need the courage to stay in the race.

6. We need to begin well and finish well.

7. We can't be double-minded. We can't have one foot in the world and the other in the Church.

8. When you have a double mind, you end up losing both.

PERSEVERE, AND YOU'LL BE BLESSED

For if any one is a hearer of the word and not a doer, he is like a man who observes his natural face in a mirror; for he observes himself and goes away and at once forgets what he was like. But he who looks into the perfect law, the law of liberty, and perseveres, being no hearer that forgets but a doer that acts, he shall be blessed in his doing. (James 1:23–25)

To talk about:

If we're honest, we can say that we all try to escape from the real world sometimes. We all try to get away from the things we know we should be doing, because some of them are hard work. What do we use to escape from the real world?

- Alcohol? There's nothing wrong with having a beer. But when alcohol starts to change who we are—when it makes us do things we wouldn't do if we were in control—then it's definitely a problem. It's taking us out of the real world, making us forget the consequences of our actions.

- Television? Again, nothing wrong with television. But if it takes up all our free time, so that we don't have any for family or church, then it's taking us out of the real world.

- Sports? A football game can take four hours to watch all the way through. If I'm spending that time with my family, it's a good thing. If I'm spending that time ignoring and neglecting my family, it's a bad thing.

- Sex? Sex is a gift from God and it's one of the greatest gifts He's given us. But it's meant to bring a husband and wife together and create a family bond. If it's pushing a family apart, it's a gift that's being misused.

GAME PLAN

1. Remember that courage is the willingness to endure an injury for the sake of the good. It's not fearlessness.

2. St. Paul "buffets the body," training himself for holiness.

ST. PAUL IN TRAINING

St. Paul, who wrote more than half of the New Testament, compares himself to an athlete in training. Like an athlete, he masters his body to win the prize.

Every athlete exercises self-control in all things. They do it to receive a perishable wreath, but we are imperishable. Well, I do not run aimlessly, I do not box as one beating the air; but I pommel my body and subdue it, lest after preaching to others I myself should be disqualified. (1 Corinthians 9:25–27)

3. Soul and body both want to be in control. The soul leads the body to heaven; the body leads the soul to hell. We need to train the body to follow the soul.

4. *Perseverance* is the ability to fight one battle after another and still hang in there.

5. Take strength from seeing how Jesus endured the Cross.

6. We have fortitude because we believe there's something worth fighting for on the other side.

7. The eternal perspective is important. We need to realize that the prize is eternal life. Our trials are slight and momentary in comparison.

8. Hope empowers courage. Hope is the confident expectation of the fulfillment of my life.

9. The power that Christ has is given to me, so nothing can stop me.

To talk about:

Let's be honest: Life is hard work. It's hard to keep on the right path and not get distracted by temptations. It's hard sometimes not to give up. But what are some of the things that can give us encouragement to persevere?

- *Family.* We love our families, and we want what's best for them. Does it help to remember how our families would be affected if we gave up or fell prey to temptation?

- *Friends.* Can we turn to friends for encouragement? Can we prop each other up?

- *Church.* Does it help to participate in church life more often? Can we draw strength from the Sacraments, from the preaching of the Word, or just from being with a lot of people who are struggling with the same problems we have?

- *Prayer.* Wouldn't it be a good idea to ask God for a little help? Remember:

> And I tell you, Ask, and it will be given you; seek, and you will find; knock, and it will be opened to you. For every one who asks receives, and he who seeks finds, and to him who knocks it will be opened. What father among you, if his son asks for a fish, will instead of a fish give him a serpent; or if he asks for an egg, will give him a scorpion? If you then, who are evil, know how to give good gifts to your children, how much more will the heavenly Father give the Holy Spirit to those who ask him! (Luke 11:9–13)

But also remember to ask for the right things:

> You ask and do not receive, because you ask wrongly, to spend it on your passions. (James 4:3)

GAME PLAN SUMMARY

Perseverance: The ability to fight one battle after another and still hang in there.

Put your soul in control! The soul leads the body to heaven. The body leads the soul to hell.

Take strength from Jesus' example: Jesus endured the Cross for all of us, because He knew the reward was worth the suffering.

Keep an eternal perspective: All our troubles now are temporary, a little inconvenience on the way to eternal happiness.

HALFTIME

The saint in training

St. Augustine, one of the greatest interpreters of Scripture, interprets Paul for us:

We're in training, Paul says.He is telling us not to treat our body as if it were the enemy, but to treat it the way a coach treats a player. It's hard work and you have to keep at it, but the training will be worth it in the end.

What he implies here is that they give up control to their bellies, and—pretending to be perfect—satisfy their own gluttony. He was working to express the same idea when he said "Food is meant for the stomach and the stomach for food" (1 Corinthians 6:13). He knows that fornication is caused by luxury, and that it leads to idolatry, so he naturally warns them against this disease often. And he sets up his own example for them, pointing out how much he suffered for the Gospel.

"It wasn't easy for me to go beyond the commands," he says ("for we endure all things"). "And likewise here I go through a lot of work to live soberly. Hunger is stubborn, and the belly is a tyrant. But I keep them under control and don't give in. I work very hard not to be led astray by my appetite.

"Don't think I get the results I want just by taking it easy. It's a race, a struggle all the way. That tyrant nature is always fighting me and trying to break free. But I don't put up with it. I keep it down, and bring it under control with many struggles."

Now, he says these things so that no one will give up the fight for virtue just because it's hard work. That's why he says "I pommel my body and subdue it." He doesn't say "I kill it," or "I punish it." We're not supposed to hate the flesh. But he says "I pommel my body and subdue it." That's the role of a master, not an enemy. He treats his body the way a gymnastics teacher treats his student, not the way someone would treat an adversary.

—Adapted from St. Augustine, Homily 23 on 1 Corinthians.

THE RED ZONE

1. Something inside us tells us we could be great. How do we do it?

2. We're made to fight—we like aggressiveness. But we run from the toughest battle—the one in the heart.

3. We like a challenge, but fear of failure tempts us to disengage.

4. Self-pity tempts us to give ourselves permission to play with sin.

5. St. Paul reminds us that we need to fight the battle all-out.

6. We need to remember that we have a commitment to be the best we can be: the best dad, the best husband, the best man.

7. Knowing you're not alone helps. Getting together with other guys helps.

8. Conversion to Christ gives us personal loyalty to persevere.

9. Living in the truth—not playing games—is the first step.

10. You need a prayer life: without it you can't make it.

    Lord, change me.
    Help me.
    I'm struggling down here.
    Please help me.

11. Talk to God the way you'd talk to a friend. Then go find friends who also talk to God.

12. Scripture is one of the biggest ways God talks to us. You meet Jesus personally there.

13. Start in the New Testament. Meet Jesus right away.

LEARNING TO PRAY

In the Sermon on the Mount, Jesus tells us how to pray. We remember the words of the Our Father, but we don't always remember how He taught us to pray those words:

And when you pray, you must not be like the hypocrites; for they love to stand and pray in the synagogues and at the street corners, that they may be seen by men. Truly, I say to you, they have their reward. But when you pray, go into your room and shut the door and pray to your Father who is in secret; and your Father who sees in secret will reward you.

And in praying do not heap up empty phrases as the Gentiles do; for they think that they will be heard for their many words. Do not be like them, for your Father knows what you need before you ask him.

Pray then like this:
Our Father who art in heaven,
Hallowed be thy name.
Thy kingdom come,
Thy will be done,
On earth as it is in heaven.
Give us this day our daily bread;
And forgive us our debts,
As we also have forgiven our debtors;
And lead us not into temptation,
But deliver us from evil.

For if you forgive men their trespasses, your heavenly Father also will forgive you; but if you do not forgive men their trespasses, neither will your Father forgive your trespasses.
(Matthew 6:5–15)

To talk about:

Let's bring our self-pity right out in the open. What do we really resent in our lives? What makes us feel put-upon? Here are some things that almost everyone has felt at one time or another.

- My family expects too much. It seems like I have to do everything in the house.
- My wife thinks if she can't see me working I must be goofing off.
- My kids never help with anything.
- I hold everything together at work. Without me, nothing ever gets done.
- Whenever the parish needs someone, they always look at me first, because they know I'm a sucker.
- I work twelve hours a day. Don't I deserve to relax?

Now let's think about some of the things that self-pity makes us do. Do we give ourselves permission to sin because we feel so put-upon?

- Do we drown our troubles in alcohol or drugs?
- Do we look for the wrong kind of sex?
- Do we let ourselves get angry at the people we love?
- Do we just sit in front of the TV when we could be doing something better with our time?

THE END ZONE

Give to God what belongs to God

You and I belong to God. Give Him your whole heart.

Life's marathon begins with one step

Turn to God in prayer.

"What do You want me to get rid of in my life? What do You want me to bring in?"

Something will come to your mind. That's God calling you.

TEMPERANCE: REMOVING THE JUNK

Brian Patrick

PRE-GAME

Temperance is a tricky virtue. All the virtues are balancing acts, but temperance more than the rest.

With courage, you know what you have to do: master your fear and do what's right.

With perseverance, it's just as easy to explain. You keep doing what's right, no matter how many obstacles get in the way.

Those are full-throttle virtues. You just go ahead and *do,* because you know what you're supposed to be doing.

But temperance is the art of saying "That's enough." Temperance goes just *that far,* and no further. It's all about controlling the throttle.

A lot of things in life need that kind of control. Pilots know how important it is to have just the right amount of power when they're flying. Too little and you fall out of the sky. Too much and you lose control.

Some famous saints have denied themselves almost every worldly pleasure. St. Simeon Stylites, for example, spent the better part of his life on top of a high pole. As long as he stayed up there, in full view of everybody but out of reach, there was no possibility of giving in to any kind of temptation.

Those great saints were good examples to us, because they proved that it is possible to discipline the body, putting it completely under the soul's control.

But not every great saint was like that, because there's nothing wrong with joy and pleasure—as long as we know where the line is.

St. Francis of Assisi is a good example. He gave up his wealth and entered a life of poverty. But he never stopped loving and enjoying nature. He called the birds and animals his brothers and sisters, and even preached to them. Everywhere he looked, he saw the beauty of God's creation. Many of us honor him with a statue in the garden, because St. Francis taught us that the joy of nature was given to us by God.

The good things in life were created to be enjoyed—but in moderation. The sun is beautiful, but too much sun burns our skin. An apple is delicious, but too many apples make us sick. Wine makes the heart glad, but too much wine makes us lose control of ourselves. Sex unites a loving couple in marriage and creates a family, but sex misused tears families apart.

Temperance is knowing where the line is, and always staying on the right side of it.

KICKOFF

1. What is a man?
   A. View pushed by pop culture: A man is unattached, aggressive, sexually charged, pleasure-seeking—experience for experience' sake. Don't deny yourself anything, and you'll have all the life you want.
   B. But Jesus is the ultimate man. If you follow Him, you will really have life.

2. Money, sex, position aren't ultimate happiness. They distract us. We were made for more.

3. Temperance: The man who has self-control actually gets it all. He's the winner.

4. The man who lacks temperance loses both eternal life and this life, because the things of this world don't give us the joy they promise.

5. Temperance is learning how to enjoy the things of this world, but not be distracted.

6. Food tastes better after you've been fasting.

7. Culture is more and more aggressively pursuing men's money through excessive sex.

ODE TO TEMPERANCE

Jesus son of Sirach lays out the sensible middle path: wine brings us joy, but too much makes us miserable.

Do not aim to be valiant over wine,
for wine has destroyed many.
Fire and water prove the temper of steel,
so wine tests hearts in the strife of the proud.
Wine is like life to men,
if you drink it in moderation.
What is life to a man who is without wine?
It has been created to make men glad.
Wine drunk in season and temperately
is rejoicing of heart and gladness of soul.
Wine drunk to excess is bitterness of soul,
with provocation and stumbling.
Drunkenness increases the anger of a fool to his injury,
reducing his strength and adding wounds.
(Sirach 31:25–30)

To talk about:

Who defines what a "man" is for us?

- Was our idea of a "man" set in grade school, where school bullies made fun of any boy who didn't act enough like a "man"? Were we among those bullies?

- Do we let movies or TV tell us what a "man" is? What messages do we get from those movies and shows about what a "man" really is?

- How about the rest of pop culture? Does popular music have an effect on what we think a "man" is and on how we think he's supposed to treat women?

GAME PLAN

1. Temperance is the ability to say, "That's enough."

2. Temperance is not prudish. God is a God of pleasure—He made pleasure for us. He wants us to have ultimate pleasure.

3. Temperance builds on prudence—the virtue that moves us to accept reality as it actually is.

4. Temperance moderates our attraction to certain pleasures so we don't undermine our becoming what we're meant to be.

5. The "flesh" is the drive toward drawing things to ourselves.

6. Prudence tells you that a woman isn't just a sex object. She's a real person: an end, not a means.

7. Women are daughters of God.

8. Self-control says, "Now that I know the truth, I'm not going to be pulled off course."

9. The flesh distracts us so that we lose the Kingdom. It's not a punishment. It's just what happens. You can't become what you're intended to be.

10. But God helps. He works inside us to produce self-control.

FLESH DISTRACTS US FROM THE KINGDOM

For all that is in the world, the lust of the flesh and the lust of the eyes and the pride of life, is not of the Father but is of the world. And the world passes away, and the lust of it; but he who does the will of God abides forever. (1 John 2:16–17)

To talk about:

What are the things that tempt us most?

- Sex? Pornography is everywhere, but even mainstream entertainment is full of sex. Let's be honest: doesn't it make us feel like we deserve the same kind of carefree, irresponsible sex?

- Food? Obviously, food in moderation is a good thing. But too much obsession with food—in either direction—can lead to all kinds of problems. If we eat too much of the wrong things, we can have health problems. On the other hand, if we worry so much about what we eat that we can't enjoy meals with friends and family, we have relationship problems.

- Alcohol or drugs? The Bible is full of warnings against drunkenness. But it also praises wine *in moderation* because it adds joy to life. Likewise, drugs can be good or bad, depending on how we use them. A little aspirin can help a headache go away and make us feel cheerful again. Addiction to painkillers can separate us from our families and destroy our lives.

GAME PLAN SUMMARY

Temperance: The ability to say "That's enough" to pleasures that might distract us.

Temperance is not prudish. Pleasure is good, but we need to stay in control.

See reality for what it is. Don't let pleasures pull you away from what really matters.

Know when to quit. Temperance builds on prudence, stopping us before we cross the line.

Let God help you. God is working inside us to give us self-control. We need to cooperate with God.

HALFTIME

Scripture on wine:

Wine makes the heart glad ...

From thy lofty abode thou waterest the mountains;
the earth is satisfied with the fruit of thy work.
Thou dost cause the grass to grow for the cattle,
and plants for man to cultivate,
that he may bring forth food from the earth,
and wine to gladden the heart of man,
oil to make his face shine,
and bread to strengthen man's heart. (Psalm 104:13–15)

... but drunkenness leads us away from God.

Happy are you, O land, when your king is the son of free men,
and your princes feast at the proper time,
for strength, and not for drunkenness! (Ecclesiastes 10:17)

Therefore do not be foolish, but understand what the will of the Lord is. And do not get drunk with wine, for that is debauchery; but be filled with the Spirit, addressing one another in psalms and hymns and spiritual songs, singing and making melody to the Lord with all your heart, always and for everything giving thanks in the name of our Lord Jesus Christ to God the Father. (Ephesians 5:17–20)

Now the works of the flesh are plain: immorality, impurity, licentious-ness, idolatry, sorcery, enmity, strife, jealousy, anger, selfishness, dissension, party spirit, envy, drunkenness, carousing, and the like. I warn you, as I warned you before, that those who do such things shall not inherit the kingdom of God. (Galatians 5:19–21)

THE RED ZONE

1. Money, food, alcohol, drugs—but the big one is sex.

2. Internet pornography is a huge industry, bigger than major-league sports. It's the biggest obstacle for young men in growing into the purity of Christ.

3. Sex is one of God's great pleasures—in the right place and time. It was God's idea!

4. But we believe the lie that it's harmless, that we can't live without it.

5. Christians aren't prudish or "obsessed with sex." The Church under-stands sex properly—it's a wonderful gift that's being abused.

6. "I got so trapped in the stuff, I hated myself"—a common testimony.

7. The one thing that's an absolute law of the kingdom of God: prayer.

8. Sin hates the light. Turn to Christ, turn to our brothers.

9. Confession: the sacrament gives us strength.

10. Ask yourself: do I really want what God wants?

11. Admit to the Lord, "I have a problem. I need your help."

12. Put God's Word in place of the garbage.

13. Accountability helps—share with your brothers.

14. Yield your life to the Holy Spirit.

15. The devil is after us. He wants to kill us. This battle is bigger than us. We need the Holy Spirit.

16. Our decisions affect our marriages, families, and friends.

17. If we give in, we give the devil access to our families.

PRAYER AND ENCOURAGEMENT ARE POWERFUL THINGS

James tells us that we should confess our sins and pray for each other. One of the best things we can do for our own spiritual lives is to help bring someone back from sin.

Therefore confess your sins to one another, and pray for one another, that you may be healed. The prayer of a righteous man has great power in its effects.

Elijah was a man of like nature with ourselves and he prayed fervently that it might not rain, and for three years and six months it did not rain on the earth. Then he prayed again and the heaven gave rain, and the earth brought forth its fruit.

My brethren, if any one among you wanders from the truth and some one brings him back, let him know that whoever brings back a sinner from the error of his way will save his soul from death and will cover a multitude of sins. (James 5:16–20)

To talk about:

Hypothetically—just for the sake of argument—if we had a problem with Internet pornography, what would help us overcome the temptation?

- Remembering our own wives and daughters? The women we know are real people, children of God like us. So are all those other women.

- Substituting real joys for false pleasures? Spending good times with the family, reading good books, just getting exercise in the outdoors—these are all things we can truly enjoy.

- Prayer? If we ask for help, Christ promises that we'll get it.

- Confession? We shouldn't forget the Sacrament of Penance. Remember that a priest who hears confessions can't be very naïve. Whatever our sins, priests have heard a lot worse. Our priests can give us good, practical advice, and the sacrament can give us the strength to follow that advice.

THE END ZONE

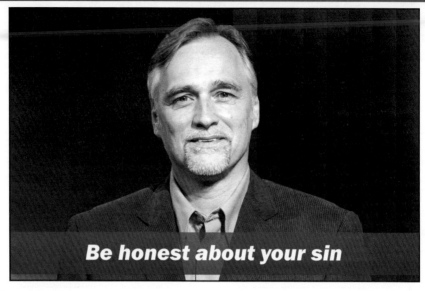

Be honest about your sin

Call sin by its name.

Ask the Lord to teach us to see sin as He sees it, so that we can be free of it.

We can overcome sin with Christ's help

TEMPERANCE:
GETTING IN SHAPE

Brian Patrick

PRE-GAME

We don't usually think of St. Paul, of all people, as a big sports fan. But he was. You can tell by the way the sports talk creeps into his letters.

"Do you not know that in a race all the runners compete, but only one receives the prize? So run that you may obtain it. Every athlete exercises self-control in all things. They do it to receive a perishable wreath, but we an imperishable. Well, I do not run aimlessly, I do not box as one beating the air; but I pommel my body and subdue it, lest after preaching to others I myself should be disqualified" (1 Corinthians 9:24–27).

Here's a man who's obviously been watching the games and—just like us—admired the men who could win the prize.

How do athletes do it? he asks. The answer: They exercise self-control. A good athlete has to be in control of his body all the time, because that's what it takes to win.

If he does anything that damages his body's ability to perform, he loses. It's as simple as that.

But what does the athlete win? In Paul's time, it was a laurel wreath; in our time, it's a ring or a trophy. And, of course, fame and fortune comes with the trophy—which was just as true in Paul's time as it is in ours.

But all those things are temporary.

Jim Thorpe may have been the greatest athlete in American history. He took Olympic medals in the pentathlon and the decathlon in 1912. He played pro baseball, football, and basketball. He got used to a life of wild applause, ticker-tape parades, and plenty of money.

Yet by the time he died, he was broke. He was taken on as a charity case for his last hospital stay. His wife had to beg for help and, ultimately, sold his remains to a town called Mauch Chunk in Pennsylvania—a town that Jim had never seen. The town changed its name to Jim Thorpe, hoping to attract business that way.

If the greatest athlete in American history was so broke his wife had to sell his body, how permanent is that "wreath" he won?

But St. Paul tells us that we're running for an *imperishable* wreath. The prize we're going for won't wither or rust. It's the greatest prize anyone could ever win: eternal life in heaven.

If a football player trains hours a day to win a Super Bowl ring, shouldn't we put *even more effort* into winning eternal life? If a runner watches every single thing he eats to make sure he can win the race, shouldn't we be *even more careful* about what we do with our bodies?

This is the big game. This is our shot at immortality. If we don't want to blow it, we have to get in shape.

KICKOFF

1. Replace junk with good things—exercise, daily prayer.

2. We were made to conquer this world and gain heaven.

3. It takes training and dedication.

4. Jesus died to make us free to change. If we're not changing, something's wrong. We haven't discovered all the good the Lord wants to give us.

5. Replace bad habits with *good* habits.

6. Cooperate with what God is doing in us.

7. Virtue isn't boring—we need to understand that Christ is an exciting leader.

8. Christ on the Cross says, "Trust me, this is the way."

WE WERE MADE TO CONQUER

What then shall we say to this? If God is for us, who is against us? He who did not spare his own Son but gave him up for us all, will he not also give us all things with him? Who shall bring any charge against God's elect? It is God who justifies; who is to condemn? Is it Christ Jesus, who died, yes, who was raised from the dead, who is at the right hand of God, who indeed intercedes for us? Who shall separate us from the love of Christ? Shall tribulation, or distress, or persecution, or famine, or nakedness, or peril, or sword?

> As it is written,
> "For thy sake we are being killed all the day long; we are regarded as sheep to be slaughtered."
> No, in all these things we are more than conquerors through him who loved us. For I am sure that neither death, nor life, nor angels, nor principalities, nor things present, nor things to come, nor powers, nor height, nor depth, nor anything else in all creation, will be able to separate us from the love of God in Christ Jesus our Lord.
> (Romans 8:31–39)

To talk about:

What good things do we really enjoy that can take the place of "junk"—the bad things that lead us away from Christ? Talk for a while about the things you really enjoy. Some ideas:

- Family time together
- Exercise
- Good books
- Hiking, sailing, and other outdoor activities
- Bible study groups
- Hobbies

How can these things help put us back on the right path, instead of distracting us from it?

GAME PLAN

1. Temperance is self-control—the virtue that allows us to say "That's enough" to any desires that get in the way of our pursuit of Christ.

2. Sometimes that means saying no, because there's a clear line.

3. If our life were a ship, temperance would be the rudder.

4. When we root out the junk, we have to replant—otherwise the weeds will come right back.

5. We've been knocked down by sin. The world is waiting for us to wake up and come alive.

6. It's not something we do on our own. The heart of the Christian life is the energy of the Holy Spirit.

7. We are created for victory. The power of hell can't stand up against us if we go on the offensive.

8. Faith is not passive. You take the kingdom by storm.

9. We want to be men of strength—men with power to accomplish good in the world.

10. With the seven Sacraments we receive the fullness of grace; we also receive the fullness of truth. Why don't we always live good lives?

11. There's a third key: supplement *grace* and *truth* with *virtue*.

12. We have a deep problem. We're more sick than we realize, since the cure is Jesus Christ on the Cross.

13. What we need is a new heart, which the Lord gives us.

IF YOU HAVE VIRTUE, YOU HAVE EVERYTHING

In a hymn to Wisdom, a poet identified as Solomon tells us that nothing does us more good than temperance, prudence, justice, and courage.

If riches are a desirable possession in life,
what is richer than wisdom who effects all things?
And if understanding is effective,
who more than she [Wisdom] is fashioner of what exists?
And if any one loves righteousness,
her labors are virtues;
for she teaches self-control and prudence,
justice and courage;
nothing in life is more profitable for men than these.
(Wisdom 8:5–7)

To talk about:

How do we "take the kingdom by storm"? And how do we take the battle to the gates of hell? What can we do to keep our faith active instead of passive? Some ideas:

*   Prayer. Even when we're standing in line or sitting at our desks, there's always time for a short prayer.

*   Going to Mass. Mass once a week helps keep us going, but there's no reason to stop at once a week. Most Catholic parishes have daily Masses.

*   Doing good works. Helping out in the church, taking care of the poor and sick, sprucing up your neighborhood—living a Christian life helps keep our minds on Christian things.

GAME PLAN SUMMARY

Temperance: Self-control—the ability to say "that's enough."

Replant after you root out the junk. If you don't plant good things, the weeds will come back.

Rely on the Holy Spirit. We can't do this alone.

Add virtue to grace and truth. We need to go on the offensive, storming the gates of hell.

HALFTIME

Root out and replant

It's good to get the weeds pulled up, to throw out all the junk that gets in the way of our road to heaven.

When we sweep everything clean, we feel better. The air seems fresh and pure, and our lives seem to be going in the right direction.

But we've only done half the work.

It's not enough just to root out the junk. If all we have is a big empty space where the junk was, something's going to fill that space.

Here's what Jesus had to say:

> When the unclean spirit has gone out of a man, he passes through waterless places seeking rest; and finding none he says, "I will return to my house from which I came." And when he comes he finds it swept and put in order. Then he goes and brings seven other spirits more evil than himself, and they enter and dwell there; and the last state of that man becomes worse than the first. (Luke 11:24–26)

The clean sweep has just made more room for junk! (Anyone who has a basement or an attic knows how that works.)

What we need to do is fill that emptiness with something worthwhile—something so strong that the unclean spirit and his buddies can't force their way in.

In other words, what we need is the Holy Spirit.

THE RED ZONE

1. The first thing is to get your personal trainer: the Holy Spirit.

2. Invite the Spirit in. The door to our hearts has a knob on the inside; we have to open it.

3. The real problem is the wounded heart. If we cooperate with the Spirit, the Spirit teaches us that we're children of God.

4. We are all prodigal sons. Our Father will forgive us, has never stopped loving us, and wants us back more than we want Him.

5. We have a spirit within us calling out, "Abba! Father!"

6. Our hearts will never rest until they rest in God, as St. Augustine said.

7. When we're touched by God's love, we can move to the next step: prayer.

8. Prayer is conversation. Talk to God the way we'd talk to a friend.

9. The first thing you do is ask, "Lord, show me how to pray."

10. The Church also gives us prayers like the Rosary and the Mass.

11. We have to have prayer in our lives.

12. Is God enough? We often see guys who look bored in church.

13. "I didn't become a committed Catholic so I could be like other Catholic guys. I became a committed Catholic Christian so I could be like Jesus Christ."

14. Our job is to wake up the sleepers in the pews by the way we live.

15. The Lord wants us to have fun. But can we complain about giving him an hour a week? Think of what Jesus went through. Can't we sit quietly for an hour?

16. The Eucharist is our power source.

17. The Father doesn't mind when we fall down—as long as we get back up and try again.

OUR HEARTS ARE RESTLESS UNTIL THEY REST IN YOU

St. Augustine wrote his Confessions—his autobiography—as a long letter to God Himself. Here, in the beginning of the book, he explains why he spent his life looking for God: because humans want to praise God, just because we're human. We were made to find God.

Great are you, Lord, and greatly to be praised. Great is your power, and endless is your wisdom.

And because man is part of your creation, he *wants* to praise you—man, who carries his mortality with him, the witness of his sin, even the witness that you oppose the proud—even man, that part of your creation, wants to praise you.

You make us take pleasure in praising you, for you have made us for yourself, and our hearts are restless until they rest in you.

Lord, teach me to know and to understand which should come first: to call on you, or to praise you. And for that matter teach me to know you, and to call on you.

Who calls on you without knowing you? Even someone who does not know you may call on you by a different name. Or perhaps we call on you so that we may know you.

"But how are men to call upon him in whom they have not believed? ... And how are they to hear without a preacher?" (Romans 10:14). And those who seek the Lord will praise him. "Seek and you shall find" (Matthew 7:7), and those who find him will praise him.

Let me seek you, Lord, in calling on you, and call on you in believing in you, for you have been preached to us.

O Lord, my faith calls on you—the faith you gave me, the faith you inspired in me through the incarnation of your Son, the ministry of your preacher.

To talk about:

It's true: a lot of people think church is boring. How can we learn to understand what's really exciting about the Mass—and keep ourselves from being bored in church? Some ideas:

• Learn more about the history of the Mass.

- Learn more about the meaning of the Mass. (Most of the words of the Mass come from Scripture. What's the context? Why do we use them where we do?)
- Read the Scriptures for the day ahead of time, and learn their context.
- Go to Mass more often—even daily.

Notes

THE END ZONE

Hunger After God

If I'm hungry, I'm going to get filled.

Say Yes To God

Nothing separates us from the heroes of the Old Testament and the saints of history, except that they said *yes* in a radical way.

The great men who endured so much for God are just like us.

WISDOM: LIVING THE TRUTH

Brian Patrick

PRE-GAME

What would you do? Imagine that God himself comes to you and says, "Listen, I'm really pleased with you. You've worked hard, and you deserve a reward. Ask for anything you like, and you can have it."

You'd probably be speechless at first. After all, it isn't every day God tells you to name your reward. So maybe God would give you a little encouragement:

"Come on, I really mean it. What would you like? A new car? A new house? Fort Knox? I can do it, you know. I'm God."

Now, what would you ask for? What would be the best and most desirable thing in the world?

This is just what happened to Solomon. You probably remember that story. He had just become king of Israel, which his father David had made into one of the important powers in the Middle East.

One night, the Lord appeared to Solomon in a dream and said, "Ask whatever you want from me."

And Solomon said, "Thou hast shown great and steadfast love to thy servant David my father, because he walked before thee in faithfulness, in righteousness, and in uprightness of heart toward thee; and thou hast kept for him this great and steadfast love, and hast given him a son to sit on his throne this day. And now, O LORD my God, thou hast made thy servant king in place of David my father, although I am but a little child; I do not know how to go out or come in. And thy servant is in the midst of thy people whom thou hast chosen, a great people, that cannot be numbered or counted for multitude. Give thy servant therefore an understanding mind to govern thy people, that I may discern between good and evil; for who is able to govern this thy great people?"

It pleased the LORD that Solomon had asked this.

And God said to him, "Because you have asked this, and have not asked for yourself long life or riches or the life of your enemies, but have asked for yourself understanding to discern what is right, behold, I now do according to your word. Behold, I give you a wise and discerning mind, so that none like you has been before you and none like you shall arise after you. I give you also what you have not asked, both riches and honor, so that no other king shall compare with you, all your days. And if you will walk in my ways, keeping my statutes and my commandments, as your father David walked, then I will lengthen your days." (1 Kings 3:6–14)

Of all the things he could have had, Solomon asked for wisdom. And because he asked for that, God gave him everything else, too.

He was right to ask for wisdom. Without wisdom—without knowing what's right—every other gift is useless. It's wisdom that shows us how to make use of the gifts we have. It's wisdom that gets us through the hard times when the other gifts seem to be taken away. All the other virtues—courage, temperance, justice—depend on the wisdom to know what's right.

KICKOFF

1. Where are we getting our wisdom? Who are we listening to? Podcasts? Television? The Lord's Word?

2. If you aim at nothing, you'll hit it every time.

3. We need to be able to ask, "Who am I and why am I here?"

4. God sent the Son to answer our questions: "I am the truth about how you should live."

5. Even if you end up on a cross, you're fulfilling your life.

6. We have to quiet ourselves enough to listen to the Word.

7. If you don't have silence in your life, you're going to miss the meaning of prudence.

To talk about:

Where do we really get our "wisdom"—what we think we know about how the world works? When we want to know what's really true, where do we get our information?

- From television news?
- From movies and TV entertainment?
- From talk radio?
- From the Internet?

Now, where *should* we be getting our wisdom?

GAME PLAN

1. Wisdom or prudence is the mother of all the virtues.

2. To be virtuous is to be the utmost we can be.

3. Prudence is the habit and skill of applying moral principles to concrete situations.

4. All other virtues—justice, courage, temperance—rely on prudence.

5. Prudence makes us look for the truth about reality.

6. It allows us to navigate life like a skier navigating a slalom.

7. Prudence asks three questions: What's just? What's brave? What's temperate?

8. Example: abortion. Panic says get rid of the problem. Prudence says the "problem" is a human life.

9. Prudence cannot deny the truth. It sees what's real, not what we want the situation to be.

10. Prudence requires listening to the truth, taking the problem to prayer.

11. Three steps
    A. Take counsel—get wisdom from other people.
    B. Make a judgment about what's right—a decision based on the truth.
    C. Take action—be bold and just do it.

12. A good man is a man of action.

13. This takes work and commitment—and we can't do it without the help of the Spirit.

To talk about:

What things in our own lives desperately need a dose of prudence? What most tempts us to panic?

- *Money problems?* Sometimes we run up debts we don't know how to pay. Jobs disappear suddenly, medical bills come unexpectedly, and soon we don't know where the money will come from.

- *Marriage troubles?* You don't have to be unfaithful to put your marriage in danger—you can do it easily enough with plain old indifference and selfishness. Sometimes we don't realize that a marriage is in trouble until it's almost too late.

- *Unplanned pregnancy?* This can be a big problem, especially for young people, both because it challenges our ability to cope and because it tempts us toward the worst kind of sin.

- *Kids in trouble?* Sometimes we don't know what's going on with our own children until a frightening phone call seems to drop the bottom out of our comfortable family. Drugs, shoplifting, pregnancy—any one of these problems with our kids can make us panic and do things we'll regret.

How do we defeat panic and let prudence manage the situation? What other people could we ask for wisdom to help us make the right decisions?

GAME PLAN SUMMARY

Prudence: The habit or skill of applying moral principles to concrete situations.

Three steps in making a prudent decision:

- Take counsel—get wisdom from other people.
- Make a judgment about what's right—a decision based on the truth.
- Take action—be bold and just do it.

HALFTIME

Wisdom from the Queen Mother

The Bible identifies this passage in Proverbs as the words of the Queen Mother. In the ancient Near East, the Queen Mother was a powerful and respected figure in the king's administration. He was expected to rely on her for good advice, and his subjects relied on her to intercede for them with the queen. In Christ's Kingdom, of course, Mary is the Queen Mother. Here, the mother of the otherwise unknown king Lemuel gives him advice about temperance. "Those who are perishing" may give in to strong drink, but we, who have a greater destiny, must always be able to make wise decisions.

> The words of Lemuel, king of Massa, which his mother taught him:
> What, my son? What, son of my womb?
> What, son of my vows?
> Give not your strength to women,
> your ways to those who destroy kings.
> It is not for kings, O Lemuel,
> it is not for kings to drink wine,
> or for rulers to desire strong drink;
> lest they drink and forget what has been decreed,
> and pervert the rights of all the afflicted.
> Give strong drink to him who is perishing,
> and wine to those in bitter distress;
> let them drink and forget their poverty,

and remember their misery no more.
Open your mouth for the dumb,
for the rights of all who are left desolate.
Open your mouth, judge righteously,
maintain the rights of the poor and needy.
(Proverbs 31:1-9.)

THE RED ZONE

1. Lack of virtue comes from lack of prudence.

2. People say there is no truth. But that's not true. Reality is real.

3. We get help with everything else, but why not with our faith?

4. Growing up means to recognize the wisdom of those who went before us.

5. We have to grow up and realize that the Church is our best friend.

6. We close our eyes and ears to the most fundamental truths.

7. We need to calm ourselves, stop and listen to the Word.

8. We are required by nature to seek out that silence so we can responsibly direct our freedom.

9. We have time for what we want. We need to make an appointment with God—schedule some time.

10. Elijah found the Lord not in the earthquake, not in the storm, but in the still small voice.

11. How do we want to pray? Ask the Lord to show us how.

12. Start with ten minutes. Or go to weekday Mass one day a week.

THE STILL SMALL VOICE

Pursued by the relentless vengeance of Jezebel, Elijah went to Horeb (another name for Sinai) to meet God face to face, just as Moses had done. Like Moses, he saw impressive demonstrations of God's power—wind, earthquake, and fire. But those things were not God. God was in the quiet voice that told him the right thing to do.

And there he came to a cave, and lodged there; and behold, the word of the LORD came to him, and he said to him, "What are you doing here, Elijah?"

He said, "I have been very jealous for the LORD, the God of hosts; for the people of Israel have forsaken thy covenant, thrown down thy altars, and slain thy prophets with the sword; and I, even I only, am left; and they seek my life, to take it away."

And he said, "Go forth, and stand upon the mount before the LORD."

And behold, the LORD passed by, and a great and strong wind rent the mountains, and broke in pieces the rocks before the LORD, but the LORD was not in the wind; and after the wind an earthquake, but the LORD was not in the earthquake; and after the earthquake a fire, but the LORD was not in the fire; and after the fire a still small voice.

And when Elijah heard it, he wrapped his face in his mantle and went out and stood at the entrance of the cave. And behold, there came a voice to him, and said, "What are you doing here, Elijah?"

He said, "I have been very jealous for the LORD, the God of hosts; for the people of Israel have forsaken thy covenant, thrown down thy altars, and slain thy prophets with the sword; and I, even I only, am left; and they seek my life, to take it away."

And the LORD said to him, "Go, return on your way to the wilderness of Damascus; and when you arrive, you shall anoint Hazael to be king over Syria; and Jehu the son of Nimshi you shall anoint to be king over Israel; and Elisha the son of Shaphat of Abel-meholah you shall anoint to be prophet in your place." (1 Kings 19:9–16)

To talk about:

The world is full of noise and confusion. Even in our own houses, somebody always has the television on, or cars with loud stereos drive by, or children run and play and scream. Where or when can we find that silence we need to listen to the Word of God?

- Early in the morning?
- Every evening before bed?
- In the nearest church?

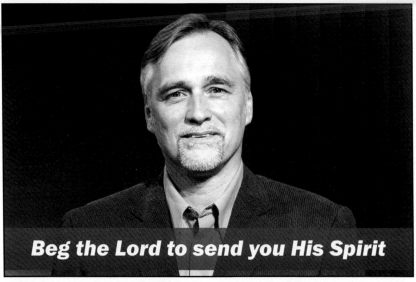

Beg the Lord to send you His Spirit

If you don't yet have the desire to do what God calls you to do, get on your knees.

Just be honest. Beg the Holy Spirit, and He'll help you.

It's time for us to grow up

Like adolescents, we don't trust those who are ahead of us.

We need to recognize that the Church can guide us.

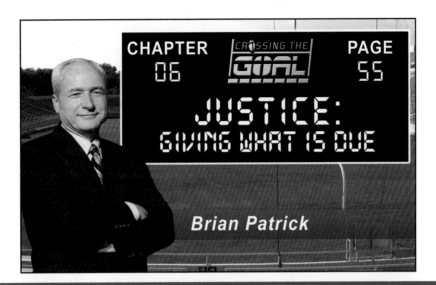

PRE-GAME

"It isn't fair!"

How many times did we say that when we were children? How many times have we said it lately?

We're born with a natural sense of what's fair—or at least a sense of what's fair to *us*.

If that were all we needed, the world would be perfectly fair.

But it's not. We're much better at deciding what's fair to us than we are at deciding what's fair to other people. When two different people have two different ideas about what's fair, we start to fight about it.

In a football game, we have rules to tell us what's fair and what isn't. There may be a lot of rules, but still a football rulebook isn't the thickest book on the shelf. It's relatively easy to learn all the rules and stick to them.

Yet we still need referees. Even when we know all the rules, we still have trouble applying them to ourselves in the same way we apply them to other people. When we have to apply the rules to ourselves, we tend to be much more generous.

That's just human nature—fallen human nature, that is. We learn to shout "Mine!" before we talk in complete sentences, but we're not nearly as good at giving other people what's theirs.

It's even more obvious when we move from football to real life. A law book *is* likely to be the thickest book on the shelf. We keep our courts busy. Sometimes the courts have to deal with someone who knew what he did was wrong. But just as many cases are about two different ideas of what's fair.

So, how do we know what's really fair? How do we develop a sense of *justice*? Where do we start?

KICKOFF

1. Begin with the Golden Rule: Do unto others as you would have them do unto you.

2. We are hardwired for justice. We have a natural sense of it.

3. The virtue of justice changes that inner sense and directs it outward. Instead of crying out, "Mine!" I cry out, "Yours!"

4. Two important questions:
    A. Do we give a person the benefit of the doubt? Or are we quick to judge that person?
    B. Do we serve others? Or are we a person who thinks, "every man for himself"?

5. The Lord redirected our instinctive gaze away from ourselves toward the other.

6. The good Samaritan is an example of Christian justice.

7. Lose yourself—stop worrying about *my* self and *my* rights—and you'll get the very things you're worried about: your self and your rights.

8. The just man goes about setting things right.

9. When we serve others, we feel a lot better.

10. The just man or woman can bring peace and order.

11. When we live the virtue of justice, we're more at home in our own flesh— we're at peace.

12. In our culture, everything seems to be "me, me, me."

13. Looking at others is the key.

14. God wants us to have glory—He'll share His glory with us, so we don't have to worry about drawing it down on ourselves.

To talk about:
Let's talk about injustice close to home. When we look in our own neighborhood, our own town or city, where do we see injustice?
- Do people live in poverty who work harder than we do?
- Does the community seem to be divided by race?

- Are there people in prison who shouldn't be? People with money who seem to get away with everything?

Try to see all these things from a divine point of view—not what's inconvenient to *me,* but what's really unjust.

GAME PLAN

1. Justice is the skill or habit of giving to others what is due to them. It's what sets things right in the world.

2. We owe the greatest debt to God.

3. Whose image is on the coin?

4. Give to Caesar what is Caesar's, but give to God what is God's.

5. The coin bears the image of Caesar. What image do *you* bear?

6. You are created in the image of God. You owe Him something: you belong to God.

7. The first act of justice is to give God adoration and thanks—to worship God.

8. God gave us two great rules: love God and love your neighbor.

9. If you're not doing one of them, you're not doing justice.

10. In the Ten Commandments, the relationship begins with God, but relationship can only happen when people do justice to one another.

11. We can never repay our debt of sin on our own.

12. On the Cross, Jesus tells us how we do justice to God. We obey Him no matter what the cost.

13. Obeying Him will lead to life.

14. Every Communion reveals that truth about how to do justice to God. We literally consume the power and life of the Lord to lead us to a transformed way of living.

15. At every Mass we experience the suffering of Calvary, but also the empty tomb.

16. If you trust Me, Jesus says, I will bring you out of this world into the world that has no end.

17. You're no fool to give up what you can't keep in order to gain what you can't lose.

18. On the Cross, Jesus opens us up to be able to do justice.

RENDERING TO CAESAR AND GOD

The meaning of this well-known story can easily pass us by. The coin belongs to Caesar because it's stamped with Caesar's image. Then what's stamped with God's image? Answer: we are.

And they sent to him some of the Pharisees and some of the Herodians, to entrap him in his talk. And they came and said to him, "Teacher, we know that you are true, and care for no man; for you do not regard the position of men, but truly teach the way of God. Is it lawful to pay taxes to Caesar, or not? Should we pay them, or should we not?"

But knowing their hypocrisy, he said to them, "Why put me to the test? Bring me a coin, and let me look at it."

And they brought one.

And he said to them, "Whose likeness and inscription is this?"

They said to him, "Caesar's."

Jesus said to them, "Render to Caesar the things that are Caesar's, and to God the things that are God's."

And they were amazed at him.

(Mark 12:13–17)

To talk about:

When Jesus tells us to give to God what is God's, He's telling us to give to God ourselves. How well are we doing with that?

- Do we really live our lives as though we belonged to God?

- Or do we try to enlist God to help us live our lives the way we want to?

- How can we know whether we're really giving God what belongs to Him?

GAME PLAN SUMMARY

Justice: Giving others what is due to them.

Give to God what is God's. That means yourself, since you are made in God's likeness.

Obey Christ, no matter what the cost. Any price—even your own life—is small compared to the prize that awaits us. "You're no fool to give up what you can't keep to gain what you can't lose."

Take your power from the source. In the Holy Eucharist, we literally consume the power and life of the Lord so that we can live out Christian justice.

HALFTIME

The Good Samaritan

We've all heard this story, but we can't hear it often enough. Jesus teaches a "lawyer"—someone who studied the Law of Moses—what it really means to be a "neighbor." (Notice that the lawyer was "desiring to justify himself"— in other words, he wanted Jesus to tell him that he was doing just fine. Jesus couldn't do that.) In the parable, the representatives of the Law, a priest and a Levite, ignore the beaten traveler. A Samaritan—an outcast— picks him up and takes care of all his needs. Christian justice goes beyond asking what's fair and instead asks what our neighbor needs.

And behold, a lawyer stood up to put him to the test, saying, "Teacher, what shall I do to inherit eternal life?"

He said to him, "What is written in the law? How do you read?"

And he answered, "You shall love the Lord your God with all your heart, and with all your soul, and with all your strength, and with all your mind; and your neighbor as yourself."

And he said to him, "You have answered right; do this, and you will live."

But he, desiring to justify himself, said to Jesus, "And who is my neighbor?"

Jesus replied, "A man was going down from Jerusalem to Jericho, and he fell among robbers, who stripped him and beat him, and departed, leaving him half dead. Now by chance a priest was going down that road; and when he saw him he passed by on the other side. So likewise a Levite, when he came to the place and saw him, passed by on the other side. But a Samaritan, as he journeyed, came to where he was; and when he saw him, he had compassion, and went to him and bound up his wounds, pouring on oil and wine; then he set him on his own beast and brought him to an inn, and took care of him. And the next day he took out two denarii and gave them to the innkeeper, saying, 'Take care of him; and whatever more you spend, I will repay you when I come back.' Which of these three, do you think, proved neighbor to the man who fell among the robbers?"

He said, "The one who showed mercy on him."

And Jesus said to him, "Go and do likewise." (Luke 10:25–37)

THE RED ZONE

1. Lying and manipulation is everywhere in the business world.

2. Truth-telling is a sub-virtue of justice.

3. We were created with a mind to know the truth about God, about us, about why we're here, about where we're going.

4. You don't come into the freedom of life unless you live in the truth.

5. To manipulate a person for personal gain by lying is a great sin.

6. Lying kills relationships.

7. Cheating in sports destroys the confidence of young people.

8. Lying lets the darkness into our souls—the darkness Christ wants to shine His light into.

9. Sin rules us all.

   A. Either we go down to greater and greater darkness,

   B. Or we turn to the Light and ask for forgiveness, mercy, and healing.

10. Christ never gives up on us, like the father in the Prodigal Son.

11. We're all living the same story. Sin rules us all.

12. Either we go down further into the darkness or we turn to the light and say, "Forgive me. Heal me."

13. The virtuous man doesn't think the ends justify the means. It's never right to do what's wrong.

14. "Do right, even when it seems right to do wrong."

15. We're made for the truth—but telling the truth is hard.

16. I'm not going to stop lying until the Lord gives me a new heart.

17. We can't run away from the truth.

18. When we live in the truth, we can begin to be just—to start setting things right.

19. When we surrender to the Lord, we get the real freedom we want.

20. The truth will set you free.

To talk about:
What do we lie about?
- Do we distort the truth to get our way in business?
- Do we cheat in games or sports?
- Do we cheat at work or at school?
- Do we say we've done work we haven't done?
- Do we cover up addictions?

Here's a chance for a real examination of conscience. Think about what you've lied about in the past, and what you're still lying about now. Maybe you lie about big things, like adultery or drug addiction. But most of us lie about harmless little things—things that hardly matter. At least that's what we tell ourselves. But even little lies poison relationships. If we can stop lying—even in the little things—and live the truth, we overcome one of the biggest obstacles between us and heaven.

THE PRODIGAL SON

Here's another story we've heard over and over. But the message is still hard for us to get. We're still tempted to shout "It's not fair!" along with the faithful son. After all, he stayed with his father and never did anything wrong, while his brother went and got into all kinds of trouble. But the father has never given up on the prodigal son—just the way God has never given up on us. God waits patiently for all of us to come back home.

There was a man who had two sons; and the younger of them said to his father, "Father, give me the share of property that falls to me." And he divided his living between them.

Not many days later, the younger son gathered all he had and took his journey into a far country, and there he squandered his property in loose living.

And when he had spent everything, a great famine arose in that country, and he began to be in want. So he went and joined himself to one of the citizens of that country, who sent him into his fields to feed swine. And he would gladly have fed on the pods that the swine ate; and no one gave him anything.

But when he came to himself he said, "How many of my father's hired servants have bread enough and to spare, but I perish here with hunger! I will arise and go to my father, and I will say to him, 'Father, I have sinned against heaven and before you; I am no longer worthy to be called your son; treat me as one of your hired servants.'"

And he arose and came to his father. But while he was yet at a distance, his father saw him and had compassion, and ran and embraced him and kissed him.

And the son said to him, "Father, I have sinned against heaven and before you; I am no longer worthy to be called your son."

But the father said to his servants, "Bring quickly the best robe, and put it on him; and put a ring on his hand, and shoes on his feet; and bring the fatted calf and kill it, and let us eat and make merry; for this my son was dead, and is alive again; he was lost, and is found." And they began to make merry.

Now his elder son was in the field; and as he came and drew near to the house, he heard music and dancing. And he called one of the servants and asked what this meant. And he said to him, "Your brother has come, and your father has killed the fatted calf, because he has received him safe and sound." But he was angry and refused to go in.

His father came out and entreated him, but he answered his father, "Lo, these many years I have served you, and I never disobeyed your command; yet you never gave me a kid, that I might make merry with my friends. But when this son of yours came, who has devoured your living with harlots, you killed for him the fatted calf!"

And he said to him, "Son, you are always with me, and all that is mine is yours. It was fitting to make merry and be glad, for this your brother was dead, and is alive; he was lost, and is found." (Luke 15:11–32)

THE END ZONE

The road to justice begins with mercy

If you're trapped in lies, trust in the mercy of God.

Turn your heart to God, and He'll set you on the right path.

Progress toward perfection

The just man sins seven times a day. You can't become perfect overnight.

God's a Father. He wants to work with us every day to make incremental progress in perfection.

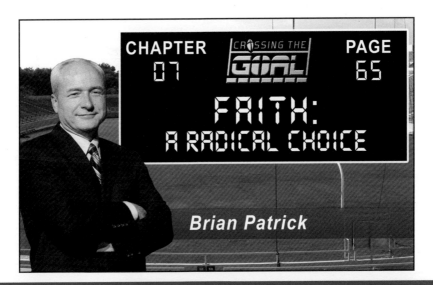

PRE-GAME

It's surprisingly easy to walk a tightrope.

If the rope is steady and you have a reasonably good sense of balance, all you have to do is just get on it and walk.

Of course, it looks a lot easier when the rope is a foot from the ground than it does when the rope is a hundred feet in the air. But the principle is the same. Just get on it and walk.

Still, it does take a lot of trust in your own abilities to get on the rope in the first place. It's one thing if it's a foot off the ground. Then nothing bad will happen if you can't make it. But if you're a hundred feet up, you'd better get it right.

The Great Blondin was probably the most famous tightrope walker ever. His most famous trick was walking across the gorge at Niagara Falls.

Of course, once he had done it, he had to do something even more spectacular the next time. He walked across pushing a wheelbarrow. He walked across with a stove, pausing in the middle to cook himself an omelet. He walked across carrying his manager on his back.

His manager recalled it as a terrifying experience, with the rope swaying all the way and the jagged rocks of the Niagara hundreds of feet below. But Blondin got him across safely.

In fact, Blondin kept up his amazing acrobatics for decades. Finally he retired and lived comfortably to a ripe old age.

You could say that Blondin justified his manager's faith in him. It certainly took a lot of faith to get up on a man's back and be carried across the

Niagara gorge, completely depending on that other man to keep you from falling to certain death.

And now you see why faith isn't always easy. You can't always just sit comfortably in your chair, feeling a kind of warm glow and congratulating yourself on your faith. That's not real faith.

Real faith demands action. It means doing things that make us uncomfortable. Sometimes it even means doing dangerous things.

That's because real faith is depending completely on the Lord—just the way Blondin's manager depended completely on the Great Blondin to get him across the Niagara. And sometimes it will be just as scary.

But we do have help. We can ask the Lord to strengthen our faith. And with that faith we can turn the world upside down.

KICKOFF

1. Faith isn't easy. We like math and science: 2+2=4. But with faith, often 2+2=5. That means it stretches us.

2. At the heart of faith is a relationship with a person.

3. Faith is to lean on that person with your whole life, in such a way that if he wasn't there you'd fall flat on your face.

4. There is a God who sent His Son to become like us, to die for us, and to rise from the dead. To believe this is absolutely radical.

5. Christianity *is* the belief in the resurrection from the dead.

6. Faith is a gift of God. But you have to work at it.

7. Once you have faith, you can turn the world upside-down the way the Apostles did. That's what the world needs.

8. The Church's mission is to spread the Gospel in the world.

9. Until men wake up to radical faith, the Church isn't going to be able to fulfill its mission.

FAITH IN THE RESURRECTION

Paul leaves no room for doubt: belief in Christ is belief that Christ was raised from the dead.

Now if Christ is preached as raised from the dead, how can some of you say that there is no resurrection of the dead? But if there is no resurrection of the dead, then Christ has not been raised; if Christ has not been raised, then our preaching is in vain and your faith is in vain.

We are even found to be misrepresenting God, because we testified of God that he raised Christ, whom he did not raise if it is true that the dead are not raised. For if the dead are not raised, then Christ has not been raised. If Christ has not been raised, your faith is futile and you are still in your sins. Then those also who have fallen asleep in Christ have perished. If for this life only we have hoped in Christ, we are of all men most to be pitied.

But in fact Christ has been raised from the dead, the first fruits of those who have fallen asleep. For as by a man came death, by a man has come also the resurrection of the dead. For as in Adam all die, so also in Christ shall all be made alive. (1 Corinthians 15:12–22)

To talk about:

Do we really have faith? It's not an easy question. In fact, it brings up a lot of other questions:

- How do we know whether we have faith?
- How would faith show in the way we think?
- How would faith show in what we do?
- Does real faith make an obvious change in our lives?
- Are we turning the world upside-down?

GAME PLAN

1. The Creed describes the content of the faith.
2. Faith is a way of knowing the truth about what God the Father has done through His Son.
3. It's a way of understanding and trusting a person.
4. God reveals His plan to us. Faith allows us to surrender our lives to that plan.
5. Many of us never come to terms with the person, and our responsibility to surrender to that person.
6. The Great Blondin as an example of faith: who's going to get in the wheelbarrow to go on a tightrope over Niagara Falls?
7. Jesus wants us to get in the wheelbarrow.
8. Why trust him?
9. The Apostles shared what they had seen and heard: He rose from the dead. Everything He said is true.

10. He tells us, "I want to give you everything you long for—life you can't lose. You can have that kind of life if you'll trust me."

11. It's a radical departure from the world, where we live a life that we can't keep.

12. The center of Christian faith is that Christ rose from the dead.

13. No one else has dealt with the problem of sin that leads to our death.

14. How do you get that radical faith?

15. Faith comes from hearing about Jesus.

16. God saves us through the preaching of the Good News—the truth that we can enter a life beyond death through our relationship with Jesus.

17. You can be preached to in two ways.
    A. Someone tells you the truth.
    B. You can read the Scriptures.

18. Ask the Lord for help when you read.

19. The Word is living: it can cut right to the core and reveal the truth of what's within us.

20. Then we must decide whether we keep living the way we have been living or follow the Lord's way.

21. "Jesus died so that those who live may no longer live for themselves, but for Jesus."

22. Christ wants to take the life we have, make it His own, and give us a new life.

GAME PLAN SUMMARY

Faith: knowing the truth about God. Faith allows us to understand and trust God.

Faith is radical departure from the world. We can surrender ourselves to God's plan.

Radical Faith comes from hearing the Gospel, from preaching and from Scripture. We know that we can enter a life beyond death through our relationship with Jesus.

HALFTIME

Faith leads to action

Do we have the faith to step out of the boat when Jesus calls us? Peter did—for a moment. Then he panicked. But he had the presence of mind to ask the Lord to save him.

> Then he made the disciples get into the boat and go before him to the other side, while he dismissed the crowds. And after he had dismissed the crowds, he went up into the hills by himself to pray.
>
> When evening came, he was there alone, but the boat by this time was many furlongs distant from the land, beaten by the waves; for the wind was against them.
>
> And in the fourth watch of the night he came to them, walking on the sea. But when the disciples saw him walking on the sea, they were terrified, saying, "It is a ghost!" And they cried out for fear.
>
> But immediately he spoke to them, saying, "Take heart, it is I; have no fear."
>
> And Peter answered him, "Lord, if it is you, bid me come to you on the water."
>
> He said, "Come." So Peter got out of the boat and walked on the water and came to Jesus; but when he saw the wind, he was afraid, and beginning to sink he cried out, "Lord, save me."
>
> Jesus immediately reached out his hand and caught him, saying to him, "O man of little faith, why did you doubt?"
>
> And when they got into the boat, the wind ceased. And those in the boat worshiped him, saying, "Truly you are the Son of God."
> (Matthew 14:22–33)

To talk about:

How do we start to form that trusting relationship with Jesus Christ that makes up true faith? Where do we get to know Jesus? Some ideas:

- Scriptures
- The Liturgy
- Other Christians

THE RED ZONE

1. Faith must be personal.

2. You have to go all the way with faith—with a personal relationship with Jesus Christ.

3. Many of us ask, "What do I *have* to do?" That's a kind of minimalism. It has no life. You're a Christian at risk.

4. Faith must be the center.

5. Christ is the ultimate coach. He'll give you eternal life *if* you commit wholeheartedly.

6. The things we believe in are *more* real than championships because they're going to last longer.

"Touchdown Jesus"
The name of this colossal mural is really "The Word of Life," but everyone calls it "Touchdown Jesus." Taking up the whole southern wall of the Hesburgh Library at the University of Notre Dame, it shows saints and scholars looking up to Christ the Teacher. From the nearby stadium, however, only Jesus with his upraised arms is visible.

7. "I didn't understand what I was missing until the Gospel opened up my heart."

8. Open that door a crack, and God's grace comes rushing in.

9. God speaks to us *personally* in Scripture.

10. Jesus says, "I'm willing to take the life you broke and give you a new life, but you need to play ball."

11. You can't shape your faith to fit *your* priorities.

12. When you really start believing, your life will not be the same. That doesn't mean it will be perfect, but everything changes.

13. Christianity is brutally difficult, impossible without God's grace and assistance, but it's good. You look in the mirror and see someone Christ died for.

14. Everything we do has a cost. One hour a week won't do it for faith.

15. We need to be willing to hear.

16. Christ will look in our hearts and tell us where we have to go.

17. Seek, and you will find—but we have to seek.

18. God puts other people in our life. Look to examples of faith.

19. The man who walks in faith is no wimp—the drunk is a wimp.

PRIORITIES

What are our real priorities? In this famous story from Luke, one young man finds out exactly where his priorities are. But there's hope even for him—if he's willing to ask God for help.

And a ruler asked him, "Good Teacher, what shall I do to inherit eternal life?"

And Jesus said to him, "Why do you call me good? No one is good but God alone. You know the commandments: 'Do not commit adultery, Do not kill, Do not steal, Do not bear false witness, Honor your father and mother.'"

And he said, "All these I have observed from my youth."

And when Jesus heard it, he said to him, "One thing you still lack. Sell all that you have and distribute to the poor, and you will have treasure in heaven; and come, follow me."

But when he heard this he became sad, for he was very rich.

Jesus looking at him said, "How hard it is for those who have riches to enter the kingdom of God! For it is easier for a camel to go through the eye of a needle than for a rich man to enter the kingdom of God."

Those who heard it said, "Then who can be saved?"

But he said, "What is impossible with men is possible with God." (Luke 18:18–27)

To talk about:

What are our real priorities? Our real priorities are the things we give precedence in our life. For example, if we can't go out to eat because there's a football game on, then football is the real priority. If we can't go to Mass because we have to work, then work is the real priority.

What things do we give precedence in our lives—things that take up our time and maybe keep us from developing our faith?

- Work?
- Television?
- Parties and drinking?

What would our lives be like if our relationship with Christ was really the top priority?

_____

_____

_____

_____

_____

_____

_____

_____

_____

_____

_____

_____

_____

_____

_____

_____

_____

_____

THE END ZONE

FAITH = RISK

Faith is a relationship with a person.

We need to make an initial decision to invite Jesus Christ to be the Lord at the center of our life—and then repeat that decision every day.

Without faith, it's impossible to please God.

Now is the time to call on Christ

COACH DANNY'S DIAGRAM:
Three kinds of people in the world

This person does not have the Lord anywhere in his life.

This person has Jesus in his life, but something else is at the center.

This person has Jesus Christ at the center of his life, and everything revolves around Jesus.

COACHING TIP
PUT JESUS IN THE CENTER

Family, job—everything revolves around Jesus Christ.

MAKE JESUS CHRIST
NUMBER ONE

PRE-GAME

If you're a football fan, you've probably heard the words "Immaculate Reception"—even if you're too young to have seen that game.

For 39 years, the Pittsburgh Steelers had been a hopeless, sad-sack team that got into the playoffs exactly once, in 1947. They lost the first game.

Finally, in 1972, they made it into the playoffs again. It was a home game in Pittsburgh, and the fans were excited to see the team making some headway at last.

The Steelers played hard against the Oakland Raiders, but it was looking pretty hopeless again. With 22 seconds left in the game, the Raiders were winning 7 to 6, and the Steelers were on their own 40-yard line.

And then the amazing thing happened. Terry Bradshaw, the quarterback, threw a long pass to the Raiders' 35-yard line. Just as the ball reached the intended receiver, a Raiders safety ran straight into him. In the collision the ball went sailing backwards, and Franco Harris, a Steelers running back, scooped it up just before it hit the ground. He ran all the way to the goal line with it.

When the touchdown was called (there was—and still is—a lot of argument about which player the ball had touched when it bounced back), Steelers fans flooded the field. It took fifteen minutes to restore order enough to play the last few seconds of the game.

The Steelers went on to lose the next playoff game, but things had changed. It was obvious that the Steelers were no longer the bottom-of-the-barrel team they had been for nearly forty years.

After that, of course, the Steelers went on to become the legendary powerhouse team everyone remembers from the 1970s—the only team ever to win four Super Bowls in six years.

But what kept them playing all those long, lean years from 1933 to 1972? What kept the fans coming back, even when they knew the team was far more likely to lose than to win?

They had hope. Maybe this season would be different. Maybe things would get better.

Without that hope, everyone would have given up years earlier. The Steelers would never have gone on to be that legendary team everybody remembers from the 1970s, because it was only hope that kept them from giving up in 1935 or so.

Now, a football game may not be very important in the big scheme of things, even if it seems like the most important thing in the world at the time. But hope is important—more important than we imagine. Without hope for the future, we'd never try to make anything better. Hope is the virtue that gets things done.

KICKOFF

1. Our Christian culture seems to be crumbling, but many still have faith.

2. "We believe—we just don't believe it makes any difference."

3. Hope lets us recognize that what we believe in can change our lives and the world.

4. Why are people losing hope? Maybe a lack of real faith in God.

5. Intermediate hopes: I hope the team wins; I hope my business does well. They're good.

6. We need the great hope: the knowledge of where our lives are headed.

7. Why is the Church losing influence?

8. Hope is not just positive thinking: it really does change us.

9. Hope is built on faith; they're inseparable. Without faith, no hope.

10. The devil wants to enslave us to the fear of death. Hope puts a knife through the heart of that fear.

ALL THINGS ARE POSSIBLE

How can we have the faith we need to have hope? This story answers that question. A father brings his son to be healed by Jesus "if you can do anything." Jesus reminds him that "All things are possible to him who believes." To that the father has exactly the right response: "I believe; help my unbelief!"

And one of the crowd answered him, "Teacher, I brought my son to you, for he has a dumb spirit; and wherever it seizes him, it dashes him down; and he foams and grinds his teeth and becomes rigid; and I asked your disciples to cast it out, and they were not able."

And he answered them, "O faithless generation, how long am I to be with you? How long am I to bear with you? Bring him to me."

And they brought the boy to him; and when the spirit saw him, immediately it convulsed the boy, and he fell on the ground and rolled about, foaming at the mouth.

And Jesus asked his father, "How long has he had this?"

And he said, "From childhood. And it has often cast him into the fire and into the water, to destroy him; but if you can do anything, have pity on us and help us."

And Jesus said to him, "If you can! All things are possible to him who believes."

Immediately the father of the child cried out and said, "I believe; help my unbelief!"

And when Jesus saw that a crowd came running together, he rebuked the unclean spirit, saying to it, "You dumb and deaf spirit, I command you, come out of him, and never enter him again."

And after crying out and convulsing him terribly, it came out, and the boy was like a corpse; so that most of them said, "He is dead."

But Jesus took him by the hand and lifted him up, and he arose.

And when he had entered the house, his disciples asked him privately, "Why could we not cast it out?"

And he said to them, "This kind cannot be driven out by anything but prayer and fasting."

(Mark 9:17–29)

To talk about:

Do we have trouble hoping? What things make us lose hope for the world?
- Abortion?
- War?
- Poverty?
- Terrorism?
- Faithlessness?
- Losing baseball teams?

How can we change our perspective on things like those and come to have real hope?

GAME PLAN

1. Hope and faith are gifts God gives us directly.

2. Faith allows me to see God's plan. It's a way of knowing the truth about what God has done in the person of Jesus Christ.

3. Hope is the deep conviction that what happened in Christ—the Resurrection—is my future.

4. Hope is rooted in the Resurrection. If Jesus Christ did not rise from the dead, there is no reason to hope.

5. Imagine that you believed in Hawaii and loved the idea of Hawaii. That's *faith*. But without *hope* you could never plan a trip to Hawaii.

7. Hope actualizes faith and mobilizes it.

8. Hope recognizes that faith makes a difference.

9. Our despair comes from not knowing where we came from, why we're here, where we're going.

10. We were made to live beyond this world. Knowing that, we can use this world in a powerful way.

11. Hope has the power to change us—to fill us with joy, courage, confidence, security.

12. Maximilian Kolbe is a powerful example of hope.

13. Hope gave Kolbe the power to step into the evil of this world.

14. Instead of madness, the Nazis heard hymns.

15. No one can take the grace of God away from us. If we hold onto it, we can walk through hell on earth.

16. With hope, I can be content in any circumstance.

17. Forgiveness plays a role in hope. It's never too late to turn around.

THE TWENTY-THIRD PSALM

Why do we hope, even when everything goes wrong? Since David's time, every generation of God's faithful people has remembered the words of Psalm 23 when things look bleak. Even though circumstances look as bad as they can possibly be, we have nothing to fear when the Lord is our shepherd.

The LORD is my shepherd, I shall not want;
he makes me lie down in green pastures.
He leads me beside still waters;
he restores my soul.
He leads me in paths of righteousness
for his name's sake.
Even though I walk through the valley of the shadow of death,
I fear no evil;
for thou art with me;
thy rod and thy staff,
they comfort me.
Thou preparest a table before me
in the presence of my enemies;
thou anointest my head with oil,
my cup overflows.
Surely goodness and mercy shall follow me
all the days of my life;
and I shall dwell in the house of the LORD
for ever.

To talk about:
Is it always reasonable to hope? How can we have hope
- when we're out of work with no money?
- when a loved one has terminal cancer?
- when we're being tortured to death in a concentration camp?

What makes hope possible even when things seem hopeless?

GAME PLAN SUMMARY

Hope: The conviction that what happened to Christ—the Resurrection—is our future.

Faith tells us the truth. By faith we know that Christ rose from the dead.

Hope is rooted in the Resurrection. Because we know that even death is only temporary, we can get through anything.

It's never hopeless. We can always turn around to Christ.

HALFTIME

St. Paul on hope.
Why do Christians have hope? When the world is full of war and suffering, when people want to kill us because of our faith, when we're out of work and don't know how we'll pay the bills, how can we hope? St. Paul gives us the answer: suffering in this world is nothing compared to the glory waiting for us. Ultimately, nothing bad can happen to us: "If God is for us, who is against us?"

I consider that the sufferings of this present time are not worth comparing with the glory that is to be revealed to us.

For the creation waits with eager longing for the revealing of the sons of God; for the creation was subjected to futility, not of its own will but by the will of him who subjected it in hope; because the creation itself will be set free from its bondage to decay and obtain the glorious liberty of the children of God.

We know that the whole creation has been groaning in travail together until now; and not only the creation, but we ourselves, who have the first fruits of the Spirit, groan inwardly as we wait for adoption as sons, the redemption of our bodies.

For in this hope we were saved. Now hope that is seen is not hope. For who hopes for what he sees? But if we hope for what we do not see, we wait for it with patience.

Likewise the Spirit helps us in our weakness; for we do not know how to pray as we ought, but the Spirit himself intercedes for us with sighs too deep for words. And he who searches the hearts of men knows what is the mind of the Spirit, because the Spirit intercedes for the saints according to the will of God.

We know that in everything God works for good with those who love him, who are called according to his purpose. For those whom he foreknew he also predestined to be conformed to the image of his Son, in order that he might be the first-born among many brethren. And those whom he predestined he also called; and those whom he called he also justified; and those whom he justified he also glorified.

What then shall we say to this? If God is for us, who is against us?

He who did not spare his own Son but gave him up for us all, will he not also give us all things with him?

Who shall bring any charge against God's elect? It is God who justifies; who is to condemn? Is it Christ Jesus, who died, yes, who was raised from the dead, who is at the right hand of God, who indeed intercedes for us? Who shall separate us from the love of Christ? Shall tribulation, or distress, or persecution, or famine, or nakedness, or peril, or sword?

As it is written, "For thy sake we are being killed all the day long; we are regarded as sheep to be slaughtered."

No, in all these things we are more than conquerors through him who loved us. For I am sure that neither death, nor life, nor angels, nor principalities, nor things present, nor things to come, nor powers, nor height, nor depth, nor anything else in all creation, will be able to separate us from the love of God in Christ Jesus our Lord.
(Romans 8:18–39)

THE RED ZONE

1. When we panic, hope reminds us that we have everything we need to face any challenge.

2. Hitting the bottom allowed Coach to start moving up. With faith growing, hope came.

3. When you hit bottom, all the lesser hopes are broken. Then you realize there is an ultimate hope.

4. Hope can start with hopelessness.

5. When we complain to the Lord, we're complaining to a Guy hanging on a cross. He understands suffering.

6. Christ is bigger than our circumstances.

7. When we hit bottom, we can admit that we aren't in control. We can relinquish control to Christ.

8. You don't have to give up worldly hopes; you just understand priorities.

9. Surrounding yourself with other people helps build up hope.

10. Accountability is key.

11. Sharing our relationship with Christ brings joy.

12. Where do you start when you have no hope?
    Ask for help.

    Ask God to come into your life.

    Ask God to send others into your life.

13. Be ready for things to be different.

PSALM 116

The Lord is the ground for all our hopes. Even in the most hopeless situation, God has not forgotten us. The words of this Psalm have formed part of Christian liturgies for many centuries.

I love the LORD, because he has heard
my voice and my supplications.
Because he inclined his ear to me,
therefore I will call on him as long as I live.
The snares of death encompassed me;
the pangs of Sheol laid hold on me;
I suffered distress and anguish.
Then I called on the name of the LORD:
"O LORD, I beseech thee, save my life!"
Gracious is the LORD, and righteous;
our God is merciful.
The LORD preserves the simple;
when I was brought low, he saved me.
Return, O my soul, to your rest;
for the LORD has dealt bountifully with you.
For thou hast delivered my soul from death,
my eyes from tears,

my feet from stumbling;
I walk before the LORD
in the land of the living.
I kept my faith, even when I said,
"I am greatly afflicted";
I said in my consternation,
"Men are all a vain hope."
What shall I render to the LORD
for all his bounty to me?
I will lift up the cup of salvation
and call on the name of the LORD,
I will pay my vows to the LORD
in the presence of all his people.
Precious in the sight of the LORD
is the death of his saints.
O LORD, I am thy servant;
I am thy servant, the son of thy handmaid.
Thou hast loosed my bonds.
I will offer to thee the sacrifice of thanksgiving
and call on the name of the LORD.
I will pay my vows to the LORD
in the presence of all his people,
in the courts of the house of the LORD,
in your midst, O Jerusalem.
Praise the LORD!

To talk about:

Do we absolutely have to hit bottom to have hope? Some ideas:

- We don't have to hit bottom if we recognize *now* that we can't go it alone.

- Maybe we've all pretty much hit bottom already, because we're all sinners.

- We don't have to hit bottom, but we should recognize that hitting bottom is often a sign of God's love and mercy. He wants us to know that we can rely on Him.

THE END ZONE

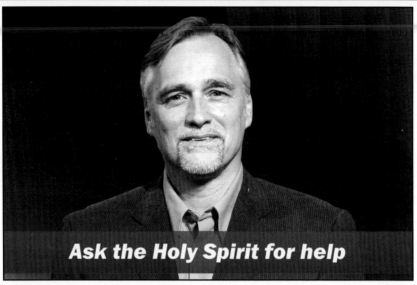

Ask the Holy Spirit for help

The hope we have does not disappoint us.

If we ask the Spirit to lead us out of our difficulties, He will be faithful.

Take God at His Word

We were made for a purpose.

God wants to build a life of hope and promise in us.

Entrust your life to God.

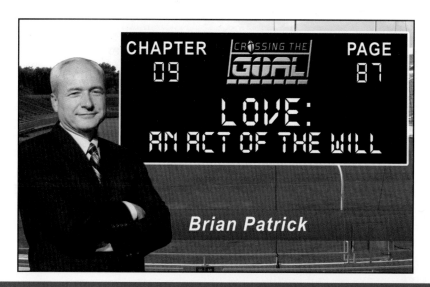

**LOVE:
AN ACT OF THE WILL**

Brian Patrick

PRE-GAME

Love is sex—that's the idea popular culture is always selling us. When was the last time you saw a movie where the romantic leads *didn't* leap into bed as soon as they thought they might like each other?

Christianity tries to tell us that love isn't just sex. So Christianity must be anti-sex, right? Over and over the message is flung at us. Christians hate sex. Christians want you not to have fun. Christians want to take the joy out of life.

For our lesson today, let's open our Bibles to the Song of Solomon. It's a book we sometimes sweep under the rug, because we don't quite know what to do with it. You may never have paid any attention to it before, but just start reading at the beginning.

A few lines in, you can already ask yourself the important question: was this poem written by someone who hated sex?

The answer, obviously, is no. Sex is good. It has to be, because God created it.

You could say, in fact, that the Christian difference is this: we know how to make sex *really* good.

We have a giant hole in our hearts waiting to be filled up with love. The trouble is that, left to ourselves, we don't always know what love looks like.

Lust looks a little like love, so we try that. It doesn't quite work, so maybe we just got the dosage wrong. We try more, and that doesn't work either.

Left to ourselves, we'll never fill that hole. But we aren't left to ourselves.

Jesus Christ came to show us what love is really like. It's forgetting about yourself and living for others. It's completely giving yourself away.

What the Bible itself dares to tell us, in that book we sweep under the rug, is that married love—complete, self-giving love between a man and a woman—is a taste of heavenly love.

Sex is a beautiful and important expression of married love. It's a complete bonding between a man and a woman who have given themselves to each other for life.

And when it happens in that environment—in a marriage, in a family, where real self-giving love is the rule—then that joy is a preview of the joy of heaven.

The key is remembering that love isn't something you *have*. It's something you *do*.

Love is an active virtue. You have to work at it all the time. But the work pays off in ways we can hardly imagine.

KICKOFF

1. The world says it's not manly to love.

2. Often men haven't received love from their earthly fathers.

3. When we miss that love, we go searching for it in all the wrong places.

4. The heart of Christianity is love—love revealed in a person.

5. God says that Jesus is His Beloved.

6. That's what we want from our own dads—an "attaboy."

7. We could blame our fathers, and they could blame their fathers, all the way back to Adam. That's original sin.

8. Christ says, "I will break this, because I am a beloved Son, with love from my Father, and I'm going to share that love with you."

9. That will bring healing and restoration to you and transform everything in your life.

10. We need that love. If we miss it, we resort to lust—using other people to fill that need.

11. If you want to receive love, you need to learn to give. Jesus gives us the power to do that by pouring Himself into us, so that we can become lovers of others.

12. The relationship of Father, Son, and Holy Spirit in the Trinity is the foundation of love.

13. Men often don't know how to receive love. It makes them feel vulnerable and weak. We don't trust love.

14. That's the evil of homosexuality. It sexualizes something that isn't supposed to be sexual—the love of a son for his father.

BREAKING THE CYCLE OF SIN

God tells Ezekiel that the people can't use their ancestors' sins as an excuse for their own troubles. God breaks the cycle of sin that passes through the generations, making everyone responsible for his own actions.

The word of the LORD came to me again:

"What do you mean by repeating this proverb concerning the land of Israel, 'The fathers have eaten sour grapes, and the children's teeth are set on edge?' As I live, says the Lord GOD, this proverb shall no more be used by you in Israel. Behold, all souls are mine; the soul of the father as well as the soul of the son is mine: the soul that sins shall die.

"If a man is righteous and does what is lawful and right—if he does not eat upon the mountains or lift up his eyes to the idols of the house of Israel, does not defile his neighbor's wife or approach a woman in her time of impurity, does not oppress any one, but restores to the debtor his pledge, commits no robbery, gives his bread to the hungry and covers the naked with a garment, does not lend at interest or take any increase, withholds his hand from iniquity, executes true justice between man and man, walks in my statutes, and is careful to observe my ordinances—he is righteous, he shall surely live, says the Lord GOD. (Ezekiel 18:1–9)

To talk about:
Did we get the love we need from our own fathers? This is a time for sharing stories:

- How we related with our own fathers
- When we really admired them
- When we wished we could have had more from them
- What we'd like to imitate
- What we'd like to do differently as fathers ourselves

GAME PLAN

1. Love is something we need desperately. Without love, violence, desperation, and anger creep into our relationships.

2. The ground of all reality is love. God is love.

3. The Christian message is that God has revealed Himself in the love of His Son.

4. It was revealed on the Cross: Jesus from the Cross tells us all, "The Father is utterly trustworthy. He will never abandon you. As bad as this looks, my Father's love will conquer."

5. He rises from the grave to proclaim, "God is love, and you're made for love."

6. God has loved from all of eternity.

7. God is everything that is good, and He has shared everything He has. That gift is so real, so complete that it *is* the Son. God's love is personified in Christ.

8. The Son gives everything back to the Father. That mutual gift of everything that is awesome and true and wonderful *is* the Holy Spirit.

9. Jesus says, "This is the life I want for you—not a life of 'What can you get?' but come in; let me give to you."

10. We're not ready for an infinite gift, because we tend to hold onto stuff.

11. The virtue of love not only changes everything on earth, but it also prepares us for life in heaven.

12. We tend to think of love as drawing things to ourselves.

13. We turn love upside-down and make it lust.

14. The real secret of love is losing yourself—giving yourself away.

15. If you want to find yourself, you have to give yourself away. The only love that will satisfy is self-donation.

16. The devil knows that we were made by and for love. He places counterfeits in our life that look and feel like love, knowing we'll reach out for them.

17. If our minds have not been formed by what God teaches us, we'll grab onto lust and think it's love—and hollow ourselves out.

18. G. K. Chesterton said that every man who has ever knocked on the door of a brothel is in search of God.

19. Christ not only can satisfy our need for love, but also heal our other relationships.

20. The Holy Spirit wants to convince our spirit that we're sons and daughters of God.

21. Every one of us longs to hear, "This is my beloved Son, in whom I am well pleased."

LOVE ONE ANOTHER

At the Last Supper, Jesus gave his closest followers a new commandment: "Love one another, even as I have loved you." When the disciples heard this, they still didn't know how far Jesus' love would go—as far as dying on the Cross.

Little children, yet a little while I am with you. You will seek me; and as I said to the Jews so now I say to you, "Where I am going you cannot come." A new commandment I give to you, that you love one another; even as I have loved you, that you also love one another. By this all men will know that you are my disciples, if you have love for one another. (John 13:33–35)

To talk about:

How did we imagine love when we were younger?

- Was it selfish lust?

- Was it a romantic fantasy of a perfect match?

- Was it fuzzy happy feelings?

What do we know about love now that we didn't know then?

- Is it always easy to love?

- Do we really get what we want from lust?

- Isn't it a lot more work than we thought?

- But isn't it worth the work?

GAME PLAN SUMMARY

Love is rooted in God. God is love.

We desperately need love. We're hard-wired to look for it. *Satan tempts us* with things that look like love, but lust never really satisfies us.

The secret of love is giving yourself away. To find yourself, you have to lose yourself.

HALFTIME

Chesterton said ...

"Chesterton said that every man who has ever knocked on the door of a brothel is in search of God."

We goofed! But only a little bit. It turns our Chesterton never said that.

G. K. Chesterton was one of the great writers of the 20th century. A Catholic convert, he was famous for pithy paradoxes—statements that seem impossible, but really conceal an important truth.

Chesterton was so good at them that, whenever people hear a good paradox, they just assume Chesterton said it. "Every man who has ever knocked on the door of a brothel was in search of God" is exactly the sort of thing he would say, and you'll find it attributed to him in hundreds of sermons, articles, and books.

Actually, it was a Scottish novelist named Bruce Marshall who said that "the young man who rings the bell at the brothel is unconsciously looking for God." According to the Chesterton scholars at Chesterton.org, Chesterton himself never said it.

But he certainly would have agreed. It's a perfectly Chestertonian paradox: it seems impossible, but it's really true. We have a hole in our hearts that needs to be filled with God's love. No matter how far off the road we go when we're looking for love, real self-giving love is the only thing that will satisfy us.

THE RED ZONE

1. There are two opposite views of love in the world.
   One world view:
   > The central meaning of life is love.
   > It's not just a feeling: it's a *decision* to surrender your life to the will of God
   > That decision will lead to total fulfillment in life.

   The other world view:
   > The purpose of life is to maximize pleasure.
   > Everything exists to be used by me for my pleasure in any way I want.
   > That second sort leads to separation, divorce, violence in marriage.

2. When we walk into a family, we bear the name of the founder of all love: Father.

3. When we abuse that name, we break the notion God's trying to give to us.

4. Nothing needs to be fixed more than that. Christianity, the Sacraments, teaching are all about fixing it.

5. Peter's experience: an argument early in his marriage. Peter blew up. While he was praying, he felt God saying, "That's my daughter. You can't talk to her that way."

6. Coach Danny: Love isn't hunky-dory all the time. You grow in love more in the trying times. When he looks at his wife, he looks through her and sees Jesus.

7. *Growing* in love is more accurate than "falling in love." Love means more than sex.

8. God gives marriage as a gift to men in particular to teach us about love. If we live outside ourselves, everything is better.

9. Many of us are filled with anger because there's something in our hearts that's not healed.

10. God says, "This is my beloved Son." We can't love until we know in our hearts that God loves us.

11. Peter's prison story: Prisoners lined up to send Mother's Day cards, but not one came for a Father's Day card. They all had broken relationships with their fathers.

12. Love is serving others, not worrying about our interests. The other person gets a big benefit, but ours is the biggest benefit.

93

13. If you show love, the love comes back to you.

14. Lose yourself, you find yourself.

15. There are people you don't like that you still have to *love*—to will their good. Love is willing the salvation of that other person's soul.

16. It's hard for men to admit they're hurting. But being honest is the key. Open up to a brother and tell the truth.

17. To tell the truth, you have to be honest with yourself.

MY BELOVED SON

At Jesus' baptism, a voice from heaven announces that He is God's own Son—and not just a Son, but a beloved Son. Our own love for our families is an imperfect image of the perfect love of the Trinity.

Then Jesus came from Galilee to the Jordan to John, to be baptized by him.

John would have prevented him, saying, "I need to be baptized by you, and do you come to me?"

But Jesus answered him, "Let it be so now; for thus it is fitting for us to fulfil all righteousness." Then he consented.

And when Jesus was baptized, he went up immediately from the water, and behold, the heavens were opened and he saw the Spirit of God descending like a dove, and alighting on him; and lo, a voice from heaven, saying, "This is my beloved Son, with whom I am well pleased."

(Matthew 3:13–17)

To talk about:

Peter Herbeck's story of the prison—where not a single prisoner had a father he cared about—shows us just how bad it can be for children to grow up without a father. But there's more to fatherhood than just being there. What does it take to be a good father? Even if you don't have children of your own, you can think about what it was like to grow up with your own father—or without him.

- How do we balance love and discipline?
- How do our children know we love them?
- How are children affected by the father's relationship with their mother?
- How do we model love for our children?

THE END ZONE

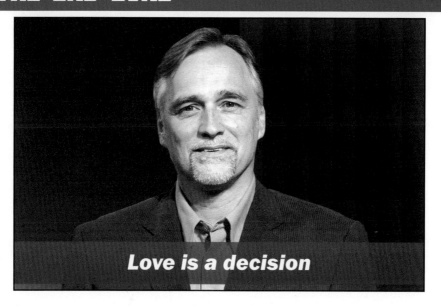

Love is a decision

1 Corinthians 13:4

John of the Cross says, "Put love, and you will find love."
We need to give love first.

Notes

Notes

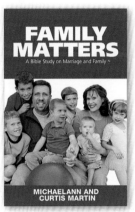
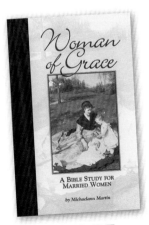

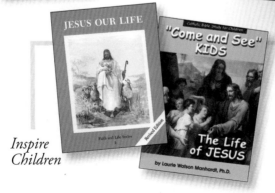

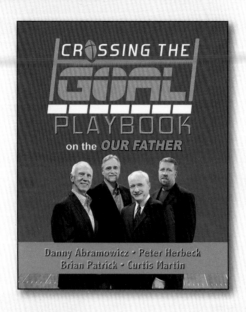